# MANUAL
# for TEACHERS, PARENTS
# and PARENT-TEACHERS

### TO BE USED WITH

## PREPARING TO RECEIVE JESUS

### First-Penance, first-Communion text and activity book

Written by a Team of Daughters of St. Paul

**In Accordance with
the New Code of Canon Law**

*auline*
BOOKS & MEDIA
BOSTON

NIHIL OBSTAT:
Rev. Richard V. Lawlor, S.J.

IMPRIMATUR:
✠ Most Rev. Bernard F. Law
*Archbishop of Boston*

## AUTHORS

The St. Paul Religion Series was produced by a team of Daughters of St. Paul of the American Province in the spirit of Reverend James Alberione, SSP, STD. The Sisters hold degrees in catechetics, theology, education, philosophy, communications and art.

THE TEAM OF AUTHORS:
Sr. Concetta Belleggia, M.A.
Sr. M. Catherine Devine, M.A.
Sr. Davina Louise Edwards, M.A.
Sr. M. Anne Heffernan, M.A.
Sr. M. Helen Wallace, M.A.
Sr. M. Mark Wickenhiser, M.A.

EDITORIAL ASSISTANTS:
Sr. Janet Peter Figurant, B.A.
Sr. Christine Robert Rimmele, B.A.
Sr. M. Gemma Stewart, M.A.
Sr. M. Clement Turcotte, B.S.

ART AND LAYOUT:
Sr. M. Charles Dangrow
Sr. Virginia Helen Dick
Sr. Deborah Thomas Halpin
Sr. Clare Stephen Kralovic
Sr. M. Alphonse Martineau
Sr. Patricia Morrison
Sr. M. Bernardine Sattler, B.A.

Printed and published in the U.S.A. by Pauline Books & Media, 50 Saint Pauls Avenue, Boston MA 02130-3491.

www.pauline.org

Pauline Books & Media is the publishing house of the Daughters of St. Paul, an international congregation of women religious serving the Church with the communications media.

This Manual is an expansion of the Penance-Eucharist sections of the Manual for "Christ Lives in Me" (Way, Truth and Life Series, Grade 2)

## At the beginning of the year's program you might like to:

— read the introduction to the program in general, as well as the specific introductions to the sections on Penance, the Mass and Communion (see table of contents).

# CONTENTS

# RELIGION TEACHER'S PRAYER

Jesus Master, make my mind holy and increase my weak faith.

Jesus, teaching in the Church, draw everyone to Your school.

O Jesus, Way between the Father and us, I offer You everything I am and have, and await my eternal reward from You.

O Jesus, Way to holiness, make me a reflection of You, the divine Teacher.

O Jesus Life, live in me, so that I may live in You.

O Jesus Life, never let me separate myself from You.

O Jesus Life, grant that I may live eternally in the joy of Your love.

O Jesus Truth, may I be light for the world.

O Jesus Way, may I be example and model for the children I teach.

O Jesus Life, may my presence bring grace and consolation everywhere.

FATHER JAMES ALBERIONE, SSP
Founder, Daughters of St. Paul

# INDULGENCE FOR TEACHING CHRISTIAN DOCTRINE

*June 29, 1968*
**A partial indulgence is granted to the faithful who take part in teaching or in learning Christian doctrine.**

*A partial indulgence is granted to the faithful, who in a spirit of faith and mercy give of themselves or their goods to serve their brothers in need.*

This grant is intended to serve as an incentive to the faithful to perform more frequent acts of charity and mercy, thus following the example and obeying the command of Christ Jesus (Jn. 13:15; Acts 10:38).

# To Parents and Teachers

This manual is designed for both teacher and parent as well as for the parent-teacher. Its aim is to foster a unified education of the Catholic child preparing to receive the sacraments of Christ's peace and love.

## Use of the manual

By means of this manual, a parent can easily note the general direction his child's classroom instruction is taking. Meanwhile, many helpful suggestions are given for reinforcing the instruction within the family environment. On the other hand, a **parent-teacher** will find that the manual's lesson is easily adapted to the home setting, if the suggested reinforcement activity is replaced by one of the alternates.

## Use of the text

The **teachers** should carefully cover the material presented in the text, pointing out and explaining difficult words, summing up the lesson, discussing the applications and summary questions with the children. (If summary answers are to be memorized, first make sure that the children understand them.)

It is important that the second grader reread his lesson at home with his **parent's** help.

## Use of the activity book

For each lesson in the text, there is a brief homework assignment to stimulate the child to read his religion book and reflect upon and apply what he has learned. The exercises are varied.

All material in the activity book is explained in the pupil text. Any adult, therefore, even if non-Catholic, can assist the child in doing his homework, if necessary.

# Chiefly to the Classroom Teacher

## The Child

In general, the primary-grade child needs the encouragement and approval of adults who are willing to accept him at his own level of development. His continued learning will depend greatly on his sense of self-confidence.

Religion appeals to him. He enjoys brief moments of silence and prayer. He likes Bible stories and, indeed, almost any kind of stories. Six- to nine-year-olds easily identify with the characters they read and hear about. This is an excellent time for them to learn more about Jesus and His close followers.

However, the primary grade child needs frequent periods of physical activity to relieve the strain of concentrating on a story, an audio-visual presentation, reading or "writing." His eyes, his muscles and his coordination are still in the process of developing. He likes to sing, to dramatize what he has learned, to draw. As he carries out these activities, he is interiorizing—absorbing and assimilating—what he has been taught. The primary-grade child learns most completely when he can be active during the learning process.

## Some Guidelines

A teacher should take a *personal interest* in his or her pupils—respecting each as an individual, making him feel accepted and important, showing interest in his outside activities.

The mother of a certain youngster noticed how enthusiastic her son looked as he emerged from his first religion class. Before she could ask how he liked it, he blurted out, "It was great! Do you know what? She knows *my name!*"

When possible, a CCD teacher might study the pupils' names beforehand. Then, during the first class period — by means of an alphabetical seating plan — one can try to associate as many names and faces as possible. Hopefully, this identification process could be completed the second week.

The classroom *atmosphere* ought to be informal and pleasant — one in which the children feel free to comment and ask questions.

Important teacher *qualities* are friendliness, understanding, impartiality and patience. This does not mean that all the children's faults should be overlooked. When a child really disturbs the class or does something clearly wrong (such as taking something that does not belong to him), he should be corrected (by the teacher), but always in such a way that his self-concept is not damaged; he should be made to understand that his action or attitude was bad but that he himself is still a person of worth.

Consistency with regard to classroom practices is a very important quality for a teacher of the primary grades.

The primary grade child learns better when we *teach only a little at a time* and repeat it often in different ways (through activities, prayers, reviews, etc.), trying to appeal more to his heart than to his reason. One main concept per lesson is enough, and it should be imparted in such a way that the child can grasp it.

At certain points it is useful to ask *questions.* Questions should be directed to the whole class; otherwise, the majority will cease paying attention. More than a simple, one-word answer should be expected, and the question should also be concrete. For example, you might ask: "What are some ways in which God shows us that He loves us?"

Answers can be received from several pupils (rather than just one) and listed on the chalkboard. If some answers are better than others, the teacher can explain what makes the others less good, always being careful not to discourage any of the children.

The children who give better answers should not be praised too much; *all* the class members should be made to feel important. (If general praise is given to all, each child will feel encouraged.)

Except during the actual presentation of the new lesson, through a story or another means, the children should be permitted to ask questions of the teacher. Every such question ought to be taken seriously and answered. Delicate questions may be referred to parents or answered truthfully but partially.

There should be an alternation of *quiet periods* with *active periods.* For example, after the child has listened to a story and looked at the pictures in his book with the teacher, he needs some physical movement— singing accompanied by marching or gestures, dancing, dramatizing, playing an active reinforcement game, or something similar.

It is good to conclude a particular stage of the lesson when you sense that the children are beginning to lose interest. However, fidgeting during the presentation of the message does not necessarily mean lack of attention; primary-grade children learn with the whole body. Likewise, the child who may be oblivious to everything around him is not necessarily bored with the lesson and ready for an activity; occasional periods of daydreaming are normal for children at this stage of development.

Give the children a chance to talk to you individually. (This can be done by moving about among them during a drawing craft activity.)

It will be necessary to check on their knowledge and understanding of prayer formulas (Our Father, Glory, Hail Mary). The mere fact that a child's lips are moving in unison with those of his classmates does not mean that he knows a prayer by heart or understands it. Shame at not knowing as much as his companions may have led him to try mouthing the words. Sometime during the year, prayers should be heard individually. If a helper is unavailable for this, you yourself might try to hear a few children during each drawing or craft activity.

## Your Guides: Christ and Mary

Jesus said:

"I am the Truth .... He who hears my word and believes him who sent me has life everlasting ... " (John 14:6 and 5:24).

"I am the Way.... He who follows me does not walk in the darkness but will have light of life" (John 14:6 and 8:12).

"I am the Life.... Abide in me, and I in you. As the branch cannot bear fruit of itself unless it remain on the vine, so neither can you unless you abide in me" (John 14:6 and 15:4).

To reach everlasting happiness with God, it is necessary to *listen* to our Divine Master, to follow Him and to *possess* His life of grace, nourished especially through the sacraments and prayer.

Show the children in practice the truths you have presented, by using examples from the life of our Lord. And never forget the value of your own Christian witness. "Christ lives in me," said St. Paul (Gal. 2:20). One little boy wanted to know what his teacher did all day long, because he wanted to understand how we act when Christ lives in us.

Your task is to give Jesus to the children. Mary gave Jesus to mankind and she continues to give Him in every age. If you want your teaching to be effective, reserve a place of honor for Mary, Queen of the Apostles, in your noble catechetical apostolate.

# Chiefly to Parents

This is a very important year in the life of your family; parents and older children have a wonderful opportunity to deepen and enrich their own faith while preparing a child for first Penance and first Communion.

## Family Spirituality

As you and your child reflect on the meaning of the sacraments—meetings with Jesus, whom we go to meet with love—you might also seek to deepen your family's spirit of prayer.

When they expressed their concern for the welfare of the Christian family a few years ago, the American bishops stated:

"Because of the primacy of the spiritual in all that makes for renewal, we give top priority to whatever may produce a sound 'family spirituality.' Family prayer, above all that which derives its content and spirit from the liturgy, and other devotions, particularly the Rosary; family reading of the Scriptures; family attendance at Mass and reception of Communion; family retreats, days of recollection and other special devotions; the observance of occasions of spiritual significance for members of the household— all these will increase the awareness of the family that it is the 'Church in miniature.'"

Perhaps this is the year to put into practice what the bishops have suggested. For example, your family might begin holding simple prayer services. Through these, religion can reach the whole child—emotions, will and body as well as mind.

Such services can be very simple, yet powerful in binding the family members closer to one another and to the Lord. A passage of the Bible may be read, followed by a homemade "prayer of the faithful" or litany, or by traditional evening prayers and a silent examination of conscience, or by the Rosary. If your family likes to sing, you could add hymns to your service. St. Augustine said that those who sing "pray double." The service may be held before a simple shrine, such as a statue or religious picture flanked by two candles. Its length should conform to the attention span of the younger children participating.

Another rewarding family activity is a "story hour," featuring Bible stories or the lives of saints. These should be told in such a way as to show God's love for His people and their correspondence—or lack of it—to His love.

The best possible environment in which a child can prepare for the sacraments is a home in which God is worshiped and witnessed to. Your role as parent will always be of the foremost importance in his religious education.

# 1
# God Loves Me

## TO PARENTS AND TEACHERS

The children may be quite familiar with the subject matter of this lesson. If so, it may be presented in the form of a review, asking many questions.

## TO PARENTS ESPECIALLY

If it seems that your child will soon be exposed to the concept of evolution (through school or through older brothers and sisters), you might wish to explain that some people think God first made all the tiny, tiny "pieces" that make up all things and that later He made trees, animals, etc., over many years by changing one kind into another. "We don't know about that for sure," you could say, "but we **do** know that without God there would be no world, no people, nothing at all. Everything comes from God."

With regard to your child's relationship with God — you own attitude can do much to teach him about his Father in heaven. If the child is treated with consistency and fairness (gently but firmly), he will better understand God's strong, unchanging love for him.

# PREPARATION

## Theme and Aim

God is our loving Father.
"I will thank God for everything He has done for me."

## Key Words

God
Jesus
heaven
hallowed

## Suggested Preparatory Reading

Genesis 1:1 – 2:25

## Materials

natural objects (such as rocks, sea shells, flowers....)
Bible
optional –

cardboard cartons, scissors, paste or tape,
old magazines, crayons or felt-tip markers

# PRESENTATION

## Introduction

*Invite the children to make the sign of the cross with you – slowly and reverently. (Turn slightly sideways, so the children will understand which hand to use and which shoulder to touch first. Otherwise, they might do it backwards.) Say the words slowly and clearly.*

Now I will say another prayer. You listen and pray it silently with me. *Pray spontaneously, briefly thanking God our Father for bringing us together to learn more about Him.*

## Message

*Play "Who Made the World?" by John Redmond, from the cassette "24 Religious Songs." Or immediately begin to present the lesson, showing your objects, pictures or slides while doing so:*

Once, a long, long time ago, there was nothing that you can see now. There was no earth, there was no sun, there were no animals and no people. It was dark everywhere, and there was nothing at all. There was only God.

And God, who is all-good, wanted many to share His own happiness. This is the reason why He made heaven and the angels. That is why He made the earth and all the people on it. Before creating people, God prepared a big, beautiful home for them. He made this whole world for all His children.

God made the sky, and in the sky He put the sun, the moon, and the stars....

God made the earth and put on it the trees, the flowers, the plants, the animals....

God made the ocean and all the fish, big and little, that are in the ocean.

God made so many wonderful things that even if we lived to be very, very old, we would never be able to see them all! Wasn't God good to make so many beautiful things!

How do you suppose God made the world?... Do you think He used anything? Shall I tell you? Well, God did not use anything to make the world. It was easy for Him to do it. He is so very great and powerful that all He had to say was, "I want this... I want that..." and, the world and all the wonderful things in it **came to be!**

## In the Textbook

*If the children are unfamiliar with the Bible, it would be well to explain what is meant by "God's Holy Book" and to show it to them.*

*Read the chapter together, making sure that the children understand who God is, who Jesus is, what heaven is. The word "hallowed" in the quotation from the Our Father may be explained as meaning "greatly respected."*

## Prayer Lesson

*Ask the children to turn to the prayer page near the front. Go through the Our Father with them, explaining each line. The words to be clarified are:*

heaven—God's special home
hallowed—greatly respected
thy—your
(This line means: "may You be respected and honored.")
kingdom—place where everyone obeys a king
will—what a person wants
(This line means: "may all people do what You want them to do"—"may they do what You want them to do on earth the way the angels and saints do what You want them to do in heaven.")
daily bread—daily food and also Holy Communion
trespasses—things people do that are wrong
*The children might be told that this is a "dangerous" line: we ask God to forgive us only as much as we forgive those who hurt us. So we must forgive others whole-heartedly.*
temptation—a thought or wish to do something bad
deliver—keep safe
evil—what is bad
amen—"I really mean it"
*Say the Our Father all together. Encourage any children who don't know it to learn it before the next class.*

# REINFORCEMENT

## Summary

God made everything. He thinks about us and loves us. He is our Father.

## Application

"Every time I think of all God has done for me I will thank Him."

## Activity for Class

Invite the children to stand in a circle, hands at their sides, and repeat after you each line of this poem with its accompanying gestures:

God made the land,   *both arms straight ahead, hands together with palms down, move them to the right, then to the left in a level manner*

God made the sea,   *move arms from left to right in an up-and-down wavelike motion*

God made the trees and birds;   *wave arms above head slowly flap both arms*

God made ME!   *point to self*

Thank You, God!   *extend both arms upward or join hands in prayer and bow head*

## Activity for Home

Help your child to make a "Wonderful World Totem Pole."

Some cardboard cartons will be needed, as well as scissors, paste or tape and old magazines. Each box is to be covered on all four sides with pictures of such creatures as rocks, mountains, water, plants, flowers, animals, birds, fish, insects, people.... Blank spaces may be filled in with words of thanks to God.

## Assignment

The activity book exercise. The learning of the Our Father if the child does not yet know it.

# ADDITIONAL AIDS AND ACTIVITIES

## At Home or in the Classroom

**Song with Gestures.** If you have the cassette "24 Religious Songs," encourage your child (or your class) to think up gestures to go with each line. These are the words:

Who made the world?
God made the world,
And all the people in the world.
Flowers and trees,
God made all these,
The land and sea—and God made me!

God made everything that's good
To show His love for us, we know.
God made nothing that is bad;
It it's bad we made it so.

Sun, moon and sky,
Angels on high,
The animals that walk and fly,
God made them all
And His praises I sing,
For God made the world and ev'rything!

By John Redmond
Published by the Daughters of St. Paul

## In the Classroom

**Film and Follow-Up.** Show "The Wonderful World God Gave Us," and have the class carry out some of the related projects described in the film guide (macaroni artwork, mobile or photo montage, prayer of thanks, creation pyramid, composition, banner).

## At Home or in the Classroom

**Dramatization.** The children may act out scenes from nature in rhythm to instrumental music—swaying from side to side like trees in the wind, curling up into a ball and gradually standing erect like seeds germinating into young plants, galloping around the room like ponies, waving their arms like birds, etc. Ask them to think of the trees, seeds, ponies, birds...thanking God for the life He has given them and showing their gratitude by what they are doing.

## At Home or in the Classroom

**Thank-You Posters.** Print the words "Thank You, God" for your child (or your class) to copy. Provide each child with a piece of construction paper and a pair of blunt scissors and place at their disposal a supply of crayons, paste and magazine clippings showing animals, plants, scenery, people. Ask each child to choose one picture that shows something he is especially thankful for. He is to cut it in a shape he likes, paste it on his piece of construction paper and copy the caption: Thank You, God!

# 2
# Baptism Is Wonderful

## TO PARENTS AND TEACHERS

The additional activity section of this lesson includes a catechetical celebration. Such paraliturgies are especially valuable because they involve the whole child, motivating him to recall something he has already learned, to see its relevance for his own life, and to respond with resolute faith through prayer, including song.

Celebrations
- combine various forms of prayer
- make the great events of salvation history present in our midst
- involve the child's will, emotions and body as well as his intellect
- create a sense of community
- deepen the child's understanding of the Eucharistic Celebration
- prepare him for the celebration of the sacraments.

## TO PARENTS ESPECIALLY

If you are teaching your child at home, try to help him appreciate the great event of his Baptism by carrying out some of the suggested home activities and paying a prayerful visit with him to the place where he was baptized.

You might also like to check on the place Baptism holds in your own life by asking yourself these questions:

- What connection is there between my daily life and my Baptism?

—Why should I be grateful for having been baptized?
—Does it seem to me that my relationship with the Father, Son and Holy Spirit is growing closer and deeper with the years?

## PREPARATION

### Theme and Aim

At Baptism we became God's children. The Trinity lives in us.

"I will be good because God lives in me."

### Key Words

Baptism
baptize
grace
soul
original sin
Holy Spirit
Blessed Trinity
heir
Church
temple

### Suggested Preparatory Reading

**FROM A GENERAL AUDIENCE OF POPE PAUL VI:**

The state of grace is "the friendship of God, the thought of God, but it is even more. It is the presence of God, a new, living, joyous presence; the presence of the Holy Spirit, who is love, who is joy, who is consolation, who is help, who is light, who is strength and courage and life. It is the living God who comes to dwell within us."

### Scripture Passages

Matthew 28:18-20
Acts 8:26-40
Romans 6:1-11

## Materials

bowl of water and suitable vessel for pouring
doll
crayons, paper, etc., for activity
*optional* —
   oil of catechumens and chrism (or the empty
      vessels)
   baptismal robe
   candle
   candlestick and matches
*alternative-*
   homemade posters showing the oils, robe and
      candle (see pp. 38-40)

# PRESENTATION

## Introduction

*If you are teaching your child at home, sit down with him at a small table on which you have placed the doll, the bowl of water and the vessel for pouring. If you are teaching a class, have the children sit in a circle around the table, so that all can see well.*

*Class may be opened with the sign of the cross and the Our Father.*

## Message

We have to drink water in order to keep alive. If you had a pretty plant and didn't water it, it would die. So water gives life. In Baptism, water gives a different kind of life — God's own life, which is also called **grace.**

The first people in the world, whom we call Adam and Eve, had God's life in their souls, but they lost it by disobeying God. Adam and Eve were our first parents. Because they disobeyed God, we were born without God's special life with us. Being born without God's grace is called being born with **original sin.** In Baptism Jesus takes away original sin by giving us God's life — grace.

In Baptism, water has a special power. Jesus Himself gives it this power. The water has this power only when it is touched to a person's head while certain words are said. These are the words:

"I baptize you in the name of the Father and of the Son and of the Holy Spirit."

Right away after this is done, a baby or even a bigger person has God's own life in him. He will never be baptized again. A person can be baptized only once.

Wonderful things happen when a person is baptized. In God there are three Persons — the Father, the Son and the Holy Spirit. They are called the Blessed Trinity. When a person is baptized, the Father, the Son and the Holy Spirit come to live in that person. With God living in us, we have become children of the Father in an extra-special way. We are **heirs** of heaven, which means that heaven will be our home someday if we are good. We are also brothers and sisters of Jesus, God's Son. And we are like churches or **temples,** because the Blessed Trinity lives in us. God lives in us. Because of Baptism, we belong to a great, big family — the family of all God's people. This family is called the **Church.**

How many things happen in Baptism! How wonderful Baptism is!

*You might show the children how Baptism is conferred. Infant Baptism is often performed by immersing the crown of the child's head in the waters of the font; if this is customary in your parish, show the children how to do so with the doll. (Tell them, however, that you are only using the doll to show them what the priest does. Baptism is only for people and children should not "baptize" their dolls or pets.) The action is repeated three times — once for each Person of the Trinity. If Baptism in your parish is performed by infusion (pouring), again demonstrate — pouring the water three times while saying the words. Let each child have a turn, provided that the class is not too large.*

*Optional —*
*Show the oil of the catechumens and chrism or the pictures that stand for them.*
Oil stands for God's goodness and the help that He gives us. Before a baby is baptized, a little oil is usually placed on his chest. This is a special oil that has been blessed. It is like a prayer for God to make the baby strong. *Demonstrate the gesture on the doll, without using the oil.* And after the baby has been baptized, a little oil is placed on the top of his head. *Again demonstrate.* The second kind of oil is called chrism. It has been given a very special blessing. It is used to show that the baby now belongs to God in a very special way.
*Hold up the baptismal robe and pass it around or show the poster that represents it. Explain that the baby receives it after Baptism. The symbolism is easily understood by children. The white robe stands for the brightness of God's life and for cleanness from sin.*
*Pick up the candle and place it in the candlestick. Light it. (Or show the poster that represents it.) Explain that the baby receives a lighted candle after he has been baptized. Usually the father holds it.* The beautiful light makes us think of God, who is bright and beautiful. We know about God and how wonderful He is. The candle stands for knowing about God and loving Him.

## In the Textbook

*Read the lesson together, making sure that the children have some understanding of what is ·meant by grace, soul, and the other key words.*

# REINFORCEMENT

## Summary

In Baptism original sin was taken away from our souls because we received God's grace. Jesus made us children of His Father, heirs of heaven, members of the Church and temples of the Blessed Trinity.

## Application

"I want to be good always, because God lives in me and I want to go to heaven to be with Him forever."

## Activity

Invite the children to imagine their own Baptism and to draw a picture of it. (Explain that their parents and godparents were present as well as the priest or deacon who baptized them.)

## Assignment

It will be necessary to explain how to do the activity book homework. **N.B.** There is one question in particular that the children will need their parents' help in answering (the date of their Baptism).

## ADDITIONAL AIDS AND ACTIVITIES

### In the Classroom

**Catechetical Celebration.** This celebration has been planned out for use in church. However, it may be adapted to classroom use by eliminating some of the parts.

The class assembles at the spot (on the church steps or in the vestibule) where the priest or deacon and members of the parish community usually welcome the infants to be baptized.

A priest, a deacon or the teacher may conduct this paraliturgy:

Here we are, right at the place where the people of our church meet all the happy fathers and mothers who bring their babies to be baptized. Let us pretend that the parents are coming now with their babies.

When the parents come with their babies, they also bring people who will help them teach their children to be good followers of Jesus. The name for these special people is **godparents.** The priest (or deacon) welcomes the parents and godparents. The parents ask to have their children baptized. The priest (or deacon) asks whether the parents and godparents will teach the children to be good children of God. Then the priest makes the sign of the cross on the forehead of each baby boy and girl. This shows that each child will belong to Jesus.

We belong to Jesus, too. Let us go to the holy water font and make the Sign of the Cross with the holy water. The Sign of the Cross reminds us that we belong to Jesus. The holy water reminds us that we have been baptized.

Now we will go into the church.

*As they enter, the children may sing a hymn they all know. Assemble the class where the parents and godparents normally take part in the baptismal liturgy of the word.*

The priest (or deacon) reads to all of us from God's holy book, the Bible. Then he explains what he has read.

*Children sit.*

*First Reading (adapted from Acts 8:26-39)*

One day a follower of Jesus named Philip was walking along a road in the desert. Ahead of him Philip saw a horse and wagon. A man was sitting inside the wagon reading God's Holy Book.

God the Holy Spirit gave Philip a good idea: "Go and catch up with that wagon."

So Philip ran and caught up with the wagon. He asked the man, "Do you really understand what you are reading?"

"No, I can't," said the man. "Someone has to explain it to me. Will you do it? Come and ride along with me."

So Philip got into the wagon and started to tell the man all about Jesus. The man was so happy!

At last they saw some water ahead. "Look!" said the man. "There's some water! Can't I be baptized?"

"Yes," said Philip. They stopped the horse and got out of the wagon. They went down to the water and Philip baptized the man. Oh, how happy the man was then!

This is the Word of the Lord.

*The class may need prompting to respond:*

Thanks be to God.

Now let us stand and say a prayer *(adapted from Psalm 34)*. The words you will say over and over are:

How good God is to us!

*Response.*

I will always praise and thank the Lord.

*Response.*

I prayed to God and He answered me.

*Response.*

I asked God's help and He gave it to me.

*Response.*

Come to the Lord and you will be full of joy.

*Response.*

God always helps people who are good.

*Response.*

Now the word you will repeat is: Alleluia.

*Response.*

God loved us so much that He sent us His only Son.

*Response.*

*Children stand.*

The Lord be with you.

*Response:* And also with you.

A reading from the holy Gospel. *(Adapted from Matthew 28:18-20.)*

*Children respond:*

Glory to you, Lord.

Jesus told His apostles, "Go out and teach everybody in the world. Baptize them in the name of the Father, and of the Son, and of the Holy Spirit. Teach them to do everything I have said you should do. I will always be with you — from now until the end of the world."

This is the Gospel of the Lord.

*Children respond:*

Praise to you, Lord Jesus Christ.

*Children sit.*

*Homily:*

We have just read two stories from God's book, the Bible. In the first story a good man named Philip taught another man about Jesus. The man asked to be baptized and Philip baptized him. In the second story Jesus told

His apostles to go out into the whole world and tell everybody about Him the way Philip did. He told them to baptize everyone who wanted to be baptized.

People who are baptized belong to God in a special way. We have already been baptized. In Baptism we received God's own life. God has given everyone who has His life the right to go to heaven. How wonderful Baptism is! How good God has been to us!

Let us stand again and pray to our Father in heaven. The words you will say are: Lord, hear our prayer.

That many babies may receive God's own life through Baptism, we pray to the Lord...

*Response.*

That all of us who are already baptized may really live as God's good children, we pray to the Lord...

*Response.*

That we may all reach heaven, to be happy with God forever, we pray to the Lord...

*Response.*

Now we will pray to Mary and the saints. We will pray like this:

Holy Mary, Mother of God, pray for us.

St. Joseph, pray for us.

St. John the Baptist....

Sts. Peter and Paul....

*The litany may be continued, by calling on the patron saints of all the members of the class.*

We have asked all our own special saints to pray for us. At a real Baptism, we pray to the special saints of the children who will be baptized.

Before the babies are taken to the baptismal font, the priest prays that the devil will go far away from the children. Then he usually puts oil on the chest of each child. The oil is like a prayer asking God to make the child strong. He also puts his hand on each child to show that God the Holy Spirit will soon come to live in him or her.

*Lead the class to the baptistry or baptismal font.*

The priest (or deacon) says some beautiful prayers, thanking God for water and for Baptism. He asks God to come to free the children from original sin and give them His own life.

After this the priest asks the parents and godparents to make their promises of Baptism again. Let us make some promises ourselves. I will ask questions, and you answer "I do."

Do you turn away from the devil?
*Response.*
Do you want to show your love for God by keeping His laws (rules)?
*Response.*
Do you know and love God our Father?
*Response.*
Do you know and love Jesus Christ, the Son of God?
*Response.*
Do you know and love God the Holy Spirit?
*Response.*

After the parents and godparents have made their promises again, the priest (or deacon) baptizes the children, one after another. What does he do when he baptizes them? *Let the children tell you.*

God our Father knows each of us by name. I will call you by name now. When you hear your name, come up to the font and make the sign of the cross with the baptismal water. *Demonstrate.* Doing this reminds us of the great moment when we were baptized.

*After each of the children has performed the action, continue:*
Every time we make the sign of the cross with holy water, we should remember our Baptism.

After a child has been baptized, the priest (deacon) takes the holy oil called chrism and puts a little on the baby's head. Why does he do this? *Wait for response.*

The baby is given a little white robe. Who can tell me what the white robe means? *Wait for response.*

The priest gives a lighted candle to the family of each child. Who can tell me the meaning of the burning candle? *Wait for response.*

After all this, everyone goes to pray in front of the altar. *Guide the children into the front pews and say the Our Father all together.*

Let us ask God our Father to bless us and to bless our fathers and mothers, godfathers and godmothers. Let us talk to God in our hearts for a few minutes....

*The singing of another hymn or "God Lives in Me" from "24 Religious Songs" may terminate the celebration. ("I Am a Child of God" from "I Am a Child of God" cassette also is appropriate here.) On leaving the church, it might be well to remind the children to think of their Baptism whenever they bless themselves with holy water.*

## At Home

**Learning through Pictures.** If your child will not be attending a catechetical celebration about Baptism, you might show him these simple pictures in your manual and read the explanation to him. Perhaps he would like to draw a bigger set of pictures for himself or make some out of construction paper.

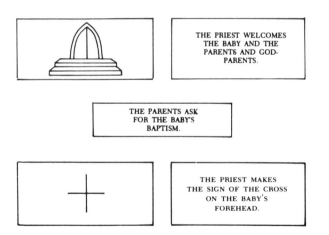

THE PRIEST WELCOMES THE BABY AND THE PARENTS AND GOD-PARENTS.

THE PARENTS ASK FOR THE BABY'S BAPTISM.

THE PRIEST MAKES THE SIGN OF THE CROSS ON THE BABY'S FOREHEAD.

*Explain that the cross stands for Jesus.* The cross on the baby's forehead shows that the baby will soon belong to Jesus in a special way. You write your name on your schoolbooks to show that they belong to you. When the sign of the cross is made on us, it means that we belong to Jesus.

EVERYONE GOES INTO
THE CHURCH.

SOME WORDS ABOUT
BAPTISM ARE READ FROM
GOD'S BOOK, THE BIBLE.

THE PRIEST TALKS
ABOUT BAPTISM.

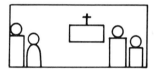

EVERYBODY PRAYS FOR
THE BABY AND FOR
THE PARENTS.

THE PRIEST ASKS GOD
TO SEND THE DEVIL
FAR AWAY FROM THE
BABY.

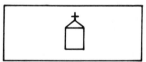

THE PRIEST PUTS OIL
ON THE BABY'S CHEST
FOR STRENGTH.

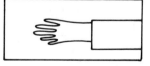

THE PRIEST PUTS
HIS HAND ON THE BABY
TO SHOW THAT GOD THE
HOLY SPIRIT WILL COME
TO HIM.

EVERYBODY GOES TO
THE BAPTISMAL FONT.

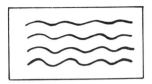

THE PRIEST THANKS
GOD FOR WATER AND
FOR BAPTISM. HE PRAYS
FOR GOD'S HELP.

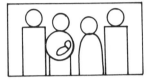

THE PARENTS AND
GODPARENTS SAY THAT
THEY WILL KEEP GOD'S
LAWS. THEY SAY THEY
BELIEVE WHAT GOD'S
PEOPLE BELIEVE.

THE PRIEST POURS
THE WATER° WHILE HE
SAYS: I BAPTIZE YOU IN
THE NAME OF THE
FATHER, AND OF THE
SON, AND OF THE HOLY
SPIRIT.

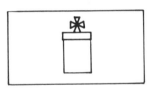

THE PRIEST PUTS
CHRISM ON THE BABY'S
HEAD TO SHOW THAT HE
BELONGS TO GOD.

THE PRIEST GIVES
THE WHITE ROBE THAT
MEANS GOD'S LIFE AND
CLEANNESS FROM SIN.

THE PRIEST LIGHTS
A CANDLE FROM THE
EASTER CANDLE. THE
EASTER CANDLE STANDS
FOR JESUS.

* Or dips the baby's head in it.

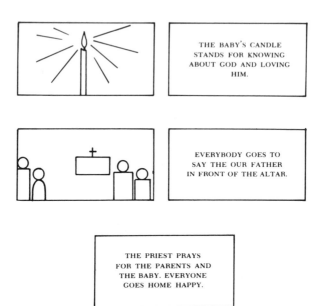

## At Home

**Candle-making.** Help your child make a baptismal candle for someone — even for himself if he does not have one. Candle-making kits can be purchased, but the candle may also be made in the following way:

Take a cardboard tube or cylinder, closed at one end. Line it with aluminum foil and stand it erect. Melt candle stubs or paraffin and pour the liquid into the container. Weight a piece of waxed string with a paper clip and suspend it from a pencil placed across the top. When the candle has hardened, cut away the container (and, if necessary, gently scrape the candle's surface to smooth it out).

Here are some symbols of Baptism that may be used for decorating the candle:

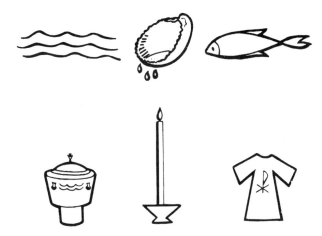

## At Home

**Banner-making.** Help your child make a large banner for his or her room. Some of the symbols given above may be helpful. (The shell is a baptismal symbol because it can be used for pouring water. The fish is an ancient Christian symbol for Christ. It may also represent Christ's follower — the Christian.) The textbook will provide ideas for the words.

## At Home

**Baptismal Reminder.** Your child could make a silhouette of himself with a baptism-related caption. Trace his silhouette (head and shoulders — profile) on white or cream-colored paper. (A single incandescent light bulb will cast a good shadow.) Have your child cut along the outline and mount the light silhouette on colored paper (receding hues, such as blue and green, are especially good). A symbol suggesting Baptism, such as a small cross or lighted candle, may be cut out and placed somewhere on the background color. You or the child may print at the bottom of the picture a few words related to Baptism that he considers especially appropriate. For a finished effect, mount everything on a large sheet of dark or neutral paper. Hang the picture in his room.

## As a Class

**Film.** Show the children the Teleketics film "Baptism: Sacrament of Belonging"—which stresses the membership aspect of Baptism. Discuss how the story of the boy is like what happens in Baptism and how it is different.

## As a Class or Family

**Attendance at a Baptism.**

# 3
# Jesus Shows
# How God's Children
# Should Live

## TO PARENTS AND TEACHERS
## —Catechesis, regarding the sacrament of Penance

The child's catechetical preparation for his first confession begins in chapter 3, which explains that Jesus came to show us how to live up to our baptismal dignity as God's children.

Chapters 4-7 treat the commandments of God simply and clearly.

Chapters 8 and 9 explain the evil of sin and the great goodness of Jesus, who died to save us.

Chapters 10-12 prepare the child to seek the Father's forgiveness in the sacrament of Penance.

Penance is a sacrament of joy—of reconciliation with our loving Father and with His people, the Church. It is a meeting with Jesus, who helps us to become better. Thus presented, sacramental confession will be an experience that the children will look forward to and want to repeat often.

When should first confession take place? The Holy See has repeatedly stated that first Penance should be received before first Communion. For example, in August, 1975, Pope Paul VI's secretary of state declared:

"The Holy Father places a special stress on confession for children, and especially on first confession, which must always precede first Communion, even if, appropriately, there is an interval between the two. From the very earliest age the first steps toward an evangelization of Penance should be taken — an evangelization which will then become an ever more valid and conscious support for a living faith in the celebration of the sacrament and, above all, in the sure and cohesive guidelines for Christian life."

Canon 914 of the New Code of Canon Law says that children should receive First Communion "preceded by sacramental confession."

It is true that the child's confession will probably be "devotional" — consisting of lesser faults. But what spiritual benefits come from such confessions!

The classic description of what frequent devotional confession does for us can be found in Pius XII's encyclical on the Mystical Body of Christ:

"By it genuine self-knowledge is increased, Christian humility grows, bad habits are corrected, spiritual neglect and tepidity are resisted, the conscience is purified, the will is strengthened, a salutary self-control is attained, and grace is increased in virtue of the sacrament itself."

A child of seven would not grasp the meaning of all this, but he should be able to understand that confession helps him to grow closer to Jesus and come closer to being the kind of person that Jesus wants him to be.

Important concepts to be imparted in the teaching of these lessons are:

— Jesus came to show us how to live as God's children.

— Jesus taught us how to love God, love others, use God's gifts well....

— He gave His life to free us from sin.

— Sin is a wrongdoing for which a person is responsible.

— Sin displeases God, hurts the person who commits it, and also hurts God's "family," the Church.

— God loves us in spite of our sins and wants us to turn to Him with sorrow.

— God forgives everyone who is sorry and wants to be forgiven.

— God's people, too, love a person who has sinned and they forgive him whenever he is sorry.

—We express our sorrow to God and His people in a special way when we go to confession.

--When we go to confession, we tell God that we intend to please Him from now on.

—In confession God forgives us and helps us to become better. We become closer friends of God and His people.

## TO PARENTS ESPECIALLY

The atmosphere of the home exerts a powerful influence upon the growing child. This special time in your youngster's life provides an opportunity for you to check on your own manner of living Christianity, by asking yourself such questions as these:

—Do I live in such a way that my children will absorb the principles of Christian morality?

—Do I create a home atmosphere in which my children can experience true forgiveness and reconciliation?

—Do I speak of God as One who always loves us and is especially pleased when we forgive, share, help...?

—Do my children see me going to confession as well as Communion?

## PREPARATION

### Theme and Aim

Jesus came to show us how to live as baptized people, who are God's children in a special way.

"I will try hard to be like Jesus."

### Key Words

example
Mary
Joseph

### Suggested Preparatory Reading

Luke 2:40-52

### Materials

Christmas crib or picture of the Nativity
crayons or paints, paper, etc.

# PRESENTATION

## Introduction

*The opening prayer could be spontaneous by parent or teacher.*

*A review of chapter two might be based on the following questions:*

When we were baptized, we received something new. What was it? (A new life. *Of course, those children who answer a robe or a candle will not be wrong either!)*

—What is the name of this special gift of God's life in us? (Grace.)

—In Baptism we became God's...what? (Children. *Another possible answer is, of course, friends.)*

—In Baptism we became heirs of... what? (Heaven.)

—What are the names of the three Persons in God? (The Father, the Son and the Holy Spirit.)

—What do we call the three Persons in God all together? (The Blessed Trinity.)

—Why should we be good? (Because God lives in us. Because we want to go to heaven to be with Him forever.)

## Message

Baptism comes to us from Jesus. Jesus is God the Son. God the Son became a little baby because He wanted to live with us. His Mother was named Mary. She was very good. His Father was God the Father. And a good man named St. Joseph took care of Jesus and Mary. St. Joseph was the husband of Mary. We call St. Joseph the foster father of Jesus. Jesus' real Father is God.

*Show the children a manger scene. Have them re-explain what you have just told them—who Jesus is, who Mary is, who Joseph is. They might also wish to talk about the other figures in the scene.*

Jesus grew up as all children do. First, He got a little bigger and began to walk and talk. Then, He grew more and learned to read, just as you did. ·After a while, He became tall and strong and He knew many things. When

He was twelve, He surprised the older people and the learned, wise men, with all the things He knew!...

In the little house of Nazareth:

*Jesus prayed.* As soon as He would wake up in the morning, He would kneel down, join His hands and pray to His Father in heaven. Do you do this, too? In the morning? ...At night? ...Every day Jesus prayed with His Mother and St. Joseph, too.... Do you pray with your family?... *Encourage prayer together. Children can be apostles of prayer at home.*

*Jesus studied.* He would listen carefully to everything the Blessed Mother taught Him.... How can you do things the way Jesus did? *Help them make the application:* arrive at school on time, do your homework well, study your lessons, listen carefully to the explanations given in class, avoid reading bad books or magazines....

*Jesus played.* All children like to play. Do you? Jesus did, too. He always played fair. He never became angry. All the other children loved Jesus! Do you think you play as nicely as Jesus did?... How do you think you could do better?...

*Jesus obeyed.* How many people were there in the little house of Nazareth?... *Name them.* Jesus obeyed the Blessed Mother and St. Joseph. He helped them in their work. Jesus always helped His parents. He was obedient. He always answered kindly.

Many boys and girls try their best to act as Jesus did all day long. When their parents ask them to do something, they remember that Jesus always said, "yes," so they say "yes," too. They help dad rake the lawn. They help mother do dishes and clean the house. They do these little chores willingly because they know that Jesus helped at home, too. When mother serves something that they do not like very much, they don't show that they don't like it. They remember that Jesus ate whatever His Mother Mary gave Him to eat. If mother and dad say: "We are sorry, but we cannot afford to buy you a bike," or something else they would like, these good boys and girls do not cry or make their parents feel badly. They remember that Jesus was poor, and that He did not have any of the nice things they have. So they say to their parents, "It doesn't matter. I am happy just the same!" How pleased parents are when their children try to be as good as Jesus was! And how happy the children are, too!

Jesus did everything well to please His heavenly Father. He loved His heavenly Father and was good to everybody.

We want to do the same, don't we? God our Father in heaven has done so much to help us get to heaven. He sent His only Son to show us the way. He Himself lives in us. We want to do our part, too. We want to know God as well as we can. We want to love Him with all our hearts. We want to do what God wants us to do. We want to be good to everybody because God loves everybody.

*Make many applications to daily life — applications which you feel are relevant to your particular local situation.*

When Jesus grew up, He went from one town to another, teaching people how to live as God's children.

Jesus taught in the fields, on mountainsides, on the lakeshore — He even taught from a boat! Many, many people went to listen to Jesus. Our Blessed Mother Mary listened to Jesus, too, and no one understood what He said better than she did.

Everyone called Jesus Master, or Teacher. What does a teacher do? What do teachers in schools do? They teach you how to read and write and do math.... Jesus came from heaven to be a teacher. He came down to teach us how to please God and go to heaven.

Jesus teaches that in heaven there is a good Father who loves everyone, who helps everyone, and who is waiting for us to share in His happiness.

Jesus teaches us how to pray, how to call God our Father. He teaches us that we must love God and obey His laws. We must keep His life in us. He teaches us to love each other and never be rude or mean.

## In the Textbook

*Read the lesson together.*

## REINFORCEMENT

### Summary
Jesus is God. He showed us how to live as God's children by obeying, studying, being kind, helping others, praying to God. He taught us to love God our Father and everybody else.

### Application
"I will try hard to be like Jesus." *Ask each child to say what he or she plans to do this week in order to be like Jesus.*

### Activity
*Invite each child to draw or paint himself doing what he has decided to do in imitation of Jesus.*

### Assignment
*Besides doing the activity book homework, the children should be ready to describe how they imitated Jesus during the week.*

## ADDITIONAL AIDS AND ACTIVITIES

### At Home or in the Classroom

**Offering Prayer.** Letter this simple prayer of offering on the chalkboard or a large sheet of paper for the children to learn and pray daily:

To God I offer all
I think and do and say.
Please bless me, O my God,
and make me good today.

Like Jesus, Your own Son,
I work and play and pray.
With Him I offer You
Obedience each day.

## In the Classroom

**Choral Dance.** *The children could be divided into groups, each of which memorizes its own set of lines. The introductory and concluding verses should be memorized by the entire class.*

*The children stand in a large circle or several smaller circles.*

ALL: *Jesus worked. Clap-clap — slowly and rhythmically. Every third child steps forward, pretends to hold up something and to hammer it.*

ALL: *Jesus played. Clap-clap. The first group of children steps back and a second group comes forward. They pretend to toss a ball from one to another, all the way around the ring.*

ALL: *Jesus prayed. Clap-clap. The third group replaces the second. The children open their arms toward heaven and look up as if talking with their heavenly Father.*

ALL: *All the time, He obeyed. Clap-clap. The children join hands and circle first right, then left. They drop hands and recite:*

Copy Jesus and you'll find
You will not regret it;
Do your duty and be kind —
God will not forget it.

ALL: *I will work. Clap-clap. Every third child steps forward and recites:*

Duty isn't always fun
Like movies, games or toys,
But when the duty's been well done
You feel surprising joys.

ALL: *I will play. Clap-clap. The second group of children replaces the first and recites:*

If friends you are seeking
They're not hard to find —

Be gentle when speaking,
To each one be kind.
ALL: I will pray. *Clap-clap. The third group replaces
the second and recites:*
When in quiet at night you kneel
And fold your hands to pray,
Tell Jesus all the love you feel
And thank Him for the day.
ALL: All the time, I'll obey. *Clap-clap. The children join
hands and circle right, saying:*
Don't be stubborn and say "no!"
As naughty children do;
*They circle left and continue:*
That word hurts your parents so,
And makes **you** sorry too.
*They drop hands and exclaim:* Jesus, I want to be like
You in all I think and say and do!

## At Home or in the Classroom

**Litany.** *On the chalkboard (or a sheet of paper) print
a response such as the following:*
HELP ME TO LOVE THEM
AS MUCH AS **YOU** LOVE THEM.
*Say the lines that change, slowly and with expression.
You might keep your hands folded as you say your own
(memorized) lines, and extend them before you, palms
upward when it is time for the class to recite the response.
The children could follow with the same gestures.
Suggested lines:*
Heavenly Father, You made all the boys and girls in
our class, and You love them....
*Response.*
Heavenly Father, You made all the people that go to
our church, and You love them....
*Response.*
Heavenly Father, You made all the men and women,
boys and girls in our city (town, etc.), and You love them....
*Response.*
Heavenly Father, You made all the people who are
black or brown, and You love them....
*Response.*

Heavenly Father, You made all the people who are white or pink, and You love them . . . .
*Response.*

Heavenly Father, You made all the people who are red or yellow, and You love them . . . .
*Response.*

Heavenly Father, You made all the people in the whole world, and You love them . . . .
*Response.*

## At Home or in the Classroom

### Brotherhood Song *

("Our Savior" is God's Son, Jesus, whom the Father sent to give us back God's life and show us what to do to reach heaven.)

SECOND VERSE:

Peo - ple who are rich,

Peo - ple who are poor—

All are meant for heav - en:

Of this we are sure.

*You might explain the last two lines briefly.*

REPEAT CHORUS

# 4
# Jesus Teaches Us To Love God the Father

## TO PARENTS AND TEACHERS

Now, in an informal way, the child begins to study God's law. He learns more about our Father's love for us and the importance of praying, of respecting God's name, of taking part in the Mass weekly.

## TO PARENTS ESPECIALLY

Nothing will better motivate your child to prayer than your own example: of praying vocally, of offering your actions to God as prayer, of accepting everything as permitted by Him.

## PREPARATION

### Theme and Aim

Jesus taught us to love our Father by praying, taking part in the Mass, and speaking of God with respect. "I will show my love for God."

### Key Words

prayer
respect
Mass

## Suggested Preparatory Reading

**FROM THE CHURCH IN THE MODERN WORLD:**

"The root reason for human dignity lies in man's call to communion with God. From the very circumstance of his origin man is already invited to converse with God. For man would not exist were he not created by God's love and constantly preserved by it; and he cannot live fully according to truth unless he freely acknowledges that love and devotes himself to his Creator" (n. 19).

## Materials

optional —
    picture, poster or slide suitable to be a visual focus of attention during a meditation on God's love

# PRESENTATION

## Introduction

*After making the sign of the cross together with the class, pray spontaneously to our loving Father in heaven. Pause, and invite the children to speak silently to God, who lives in them.*

*Then ask some questions based on the most recent activity book assignment. Stress the prayerfulness of Jesus, thus leading into today's theme.*

Prayer means talking with God, who loves us more than anyone else in the world does. *Discuss some natural gifts that the children have probably taken for granted — life, health, energy.... Talk about some of the beautiful things the people of your city or town may all enjoy. (Try to refer only to what all the children have access to.)* All of these are signs of God's love for us.

## Message

*If the children have been attentive, guide them in a brief meditation (about two minutes long). They may put their heads down on their desks or look at a picture* that you have brought in because of its appropriateness for the prayer theme. Moving to the back of the room, speak softly, reviewing the beautiful signs of God's love that you have just discussed, recalling His desire to share His own happiness with us in heaven, and inviting the children to silently thank Him for His goodness.

Explain that this is a way of praying, of talking to God, and that it pleases Him very much.

## In the Textbook

Read lesson four slowly and carefully, explaining that God our Father will help us to reach heaven if we do what Jesus asks of us. Jesus asks us to talk with our Father in prayer, to speak of Him with respect, and to pray to Him with others at Mass every Sunday (or Saturday evening).

# REINFORCEMENT

## Summary

God our Father loves us very much—more than anyone else in the world does. He wants us to be happy in heaven. Jesus taught us to love our Father by talking to Him in prayer, speaking of Him with respect, and praying with others at Mass.

## Application

Ask each child to say what he or she especially plans to do this week to show his or her love for God.

## Activity

If possible, take the children on a tour of the parish church, first impressing on them the need to be very quiet and respectful, because the church is the house of God.

At the church door, remind them that they are about to enter the house of God. Lead them into the vestibule and pause at the holy water font.

Before we go into the church we dip our fingers into the holy water. The holy water is here to make us think of the day we were baptized with water. That was the day we became children of God in a special way and members of the wonderful family of God we call the Church. We make the sign of the cross with the holy water. The sign of the cross is a special sign of the followers of Jesus.

*Lead the children into the church and gather them together before the tabernacle for an Our Father or spontaneous prayer. Explain that Jesus is truly present in the tabernacle, and show them how to genuflect "as a sign of our respect."*

*Then take the children through the church slowly. You will especially want to explain about the sanctuary, the altar, the tabernacle, the sanctuary lamp, the baptismal font, the organ, the stations of the cross, the statues and who they represent, the messages conveyed by the stained-glass windows.*

*You will probably want to show them the confessional (all compartments) and the reconciliation room and explain a little about what they will do when going to confession.*

*During this visit, it would be well to review the key points of the lesson, namely—*
*— God's love for us*
*— the importance of talking with Him, of speaking of Him with respect, of praying at Mass.*

*It is important for your pupils to feel that they belong in the church. Familiarity with the church furnishings and decorations will lead them in this direction.*

*Try to maintain an atmosphere of joyful reverence throughout the visit, which could be terminated by another prayer before the Blessed Sacrament.*

## Assignment

*The activity-book exercises should be explained carefully.*

## ADDITIONAL AIDS AND ACTIVITIES

### *At Home*

**Prayer Corner.** Help the child choose a suitable spot for his or her own prayer corner, or for that of the whole family. Some devotional object will be needed — for example, a crucifix, a statue or a holy picture. Encourage him to spend at least a few minutes a day talking with God. Also point out that he can pray *anywhere,* at any time, even though certain times and places are *especially* important.

### *At Home or in the Classroom*

**Glory to the Father....** In keeping with this lesson's spirit of love and gratitude, teach the children the "Glory," reviewing the names of the Persons of the Trinity and explaining that in this prayer we say we want God to be praised as He always has been and always will be.

# 5
# Jesus Teaches Us To Love One Another

## TO PARENTS AND TEACHERS

This lesson is an informal introduction to the fourth and fifth commandments, with emphasis on the positive aspects of both. (The negative aspects will be treated in the chapters on sin and confession.)

## PREPARATION

### Theme and Aim

Jesus asks us to love everybody.
"I will be kind to everyone."

### Key Words

help
share
obey
neighbor

### Suggested Preparatory Reading

**FROM THE CHURCH IN THE MODERN WORLD:**
"God, who has fatherly concern for everyone, has willed that all men should constitute one family and treat

one another in a spirit of brotherhood. For having been created in the image of God, who 'from one man has created the whole human race and made them live all over the face of the earth' (Acts 17:26), all men are called to one and the same goal, namely, God Himself.

"For this reason, love for God and neighbor is the first and greatest commandment. Sacred Scripture, however, teaches us that the love of God cannot be separated from love of neighbor: 'If there is any other commandment, it is summed up in this saying: You shall love your neighbor as yourself.... Love therefore is the fulfillment of the Law' (Rom. 13:9-10; cf. 1 Jn. 4:20)." (n. 24)

## Materials

poster, bulletin board or flannelboard described under "Message," crayons or paints, paper, etc.
*optional* —
visuals to illustrate the parable of the good Samaritan
*alternative* —
a picture of Jesus

## PRESENTATION

### Introduction

*Encourage spontaneous prayer by class members:*
After we make the sign of the cross, we will all be quiet. Then anyone who would like to make up a little prayer may say it out loud....

*Discuss how the children carried out their resolutions about showing their love for God.*

### Message

*Display a poster, bulletin board or flannelboard with pictures of adults helping children or playing with them.*
We have talked about several ways in which God shows His love for us. One very special way is through other people, the people who take care of us.

*N.B. — The examples given here will depend on the home situation of each member of your class. If some seem to have emotional problems which suggest a poor home environment, it would be well to be very general, speaking of mother or father, teachers, doctors, policemen, etc. If, instead, you know that each of the children has a loving parent or guardian, you could mention each one as an example:* Janie's mother, Billy's foster mother, Mrs. Thompson, Kevin's parents....

God shows His love for us through these people, and another way we can show our love for God is by loving them back. We can show our love for God by obeying them and helping them.

*Discuss concrete ways a boy or girl can show love for parents, foster parents, classroom teachers, etc. How can they help? In what other ways can they show love?*

Jesus asks us to be good to other people, too. Would you like to hear one of the most beautiful stories Jesus ever told?

*Display a picture of Jesus, as if He were telling the story in person, or — if you have the possibility — accompany your good Samaritan narrative with a visual presentation (sketches, flannelboard, figures, a filmstrip....)*

One day a man asked Jesus, "What should I do so I can go to heaven?"

Jesus answered the man by asking him a question. "What does God's Book say?" He asked.

The man knew God's Book well. So he knew what to answer. "It tells us to love God with our whole heart and soul and strength and mind," he said. "And God's Book also says to love our neighbor as much as we love ourselves."

"Good," said Jesus. "Do this and you will go to heaven."

"But I'm not sure who my neighbor is," said the man.

*Write the word NEIGHBOR on the chalkboard or a sheet of paper.*

"I'll tell you a story," said Jesus. "Then you will be sure who your neighbor is."

So Jesus told a story. There were several people in the story. Most of the people were *Jews.* They belonged to one country. Only one person in the story belonged to another country. He was a *Samaritan.* Usually Jews did not like Samaritans and Samaritans did not like Jews.

The story that Jesus told was something like this:

One day a Jewish man was riding his donkey down a steep, rocky road. He was going from one city to another, and he had some money with him.

That road was very dangerous. There were big rocks alongside it, and often robbers would hide behind those rocks until they saw someone coming by.

That was what happened now. A group of robbers came out from behind some rocks. Before the poor man could do anything, the robbers grabbed his donkey. Then they pulled the man off the donkey and took his money. They even took his clothes. Then they beat and beat him with sticks. After that they left the poor man by the roadside to die.

The man lay there beside the road. He couldn't do anything. He hurt so terribly that he couldn't move. He couldn't even think. He just lay there.

After a while an important person came riding down the rocky road. This important man saw the man who had been hurt. But he pretended that he *didn't* see him. He did not want to take time to help someone else. So he rode right on by.

Then another man came along. He was not as important as the first man. But he kept on going, too. He didn't want to stop and help either.

At last a third man came riding down the road. This man was a Samaritan, and usually Samaritans were not liked by Jewish people. As soon as the Samaritan saw the poor Jewish man in the ditch, he stopped his donkey and got off. He looked at the man who had been hurt and saw that he was still alive. "I'll help you," said the Samaritan. He had some oil and wine with him. These were good for making sores get better. He poured the oil and wine on the man's cuts and sores. Then he tore up some of his own clothes to make bandages. After that, he picked up the man who had been hurt and put him on his own donkey. He tied him so he wouldn't fall. Then he walked alongside the donkey all the way to the nearest hotel.

There weren't any hospitals in those days. So the Samaritan asked the hotel owner to take care of the man who was hurt. "Here's some money," he said. "Give him good care. If you have to spend more money than what I gave you, spend it, and I'll pay you back. I have to leave now, but in a few days I'll be back to see how everything is." *Pause for a few moments.*

That was the end of Jesus' story. After He had finished, Jesus looked at the man who had wanted to know who his neighbor was.

Jesus asked, "Which of the people in this story was a neighbor to the man who was hurt?"

What do you think the answer is, boys and girls? *Wait for response.*

That's just what the man answered, too. And then Jesus said, "Go and act the same way."

*Discuss how the children can help others who need help — new students, their younger brothers and sisters.... Make sure, however, that they realize they must be careful in their dealings with strangers.*

## In the Textbook

*Read lesson 5 together.*

## REINFORCEMENT

### Summary

Jesus asks us to show our love for God by loving everybody, especially the people who are closest to us. He asks us to be kind to everyone.

### Application

*Invite each child to tell what he or she will do to show love and kindness towards someone.*

## Activity

Turn to the prayer-poem "We Want To Love God" in the activity book (beginning of the poem and song section). Recite it together with the children or divide the class into two groups and have them alternate lines. Invite each child to draw or paint a picture about one of the lines in the poem.

## Assignment

The picture-study exercise might be done together, during the class period.

# ADDITIONAL AIDS AND ACTIVITIES

## In the Classroom

**Dramatization** — The good Samaritan. *The following is merely a guide. The children should be encouraged to use their own words.*
*Narrator:* Jesus loved to tell people about God our Father. And when they asked Him questions, He would answer them with kindness.
*Jesus enters with the lawyer.*
*Lawyer:* Master, what must I do to win everlasting life?
*Jesus:* What is written in the Holy Book? What do you read in it?
*Lawyer:* You shall love the Lord your God with your whole heart and with your whole soul and with your whole strength and with your whole mind, and you shall love your neighbor as yourself.
*Jesus:* You have answered well. Do this and you will live.
*Lawyer:* But tell me, Master, who is my neighbor?
*Jesus:* There was a man going from Jerusalem to Jericho. He was attacked by robbers, who beat him and left him half dead . . . .
*Off to one side, three children (gently) act out this scene.*

*Jesus:* Now, an important man happened to be coming by, but when he saw the poor man, he kept on going.
*The man walks across the "stage."*
*Jesus:* Then another man came by. He, too, saw the poor man who had been beaten, but he kept on going.
*The second man walks through.*
*Jesus:* But a Samaritan was traveling by . . .
*The Samaritan enters and kneels down beside the victim.*
*Samaritan:* Who has done this to you? I feel sorry for you even though I do not know you. Poor man! I have some oil and wine. I'll pour them on your wounds and bandage them up.
*He binds up the wounds.*
*Samaritan:* Now I will take you to the nearest hotel so that someone can take care of you.
*Jesus:* So the Samaritan lifted up the man and put him on his own donkey and took him to the nearest hotel.
*Samaritan (to the innkeeper):* Here is some money. I have to go now, but take care of him. When I come back I'll pay you back for anything extra you spend on him.
*Jesus (turning to the lawyer):* Which of these three men do you think was a neighbor to the man who was beaten by the robbers?
*Lawyer:* The man who felt sorry for him and helped him.
*Jesus:* Go, and do the same thing.

*The children gather in a circle, hold hands and sing the "Brotherhood Song" (suggested in conjunction with lesson 3).*

## At Home or in the Classroom

**Another story:** Near the city of Catania in Southern Italy is a volcano, which sometimes sends out steaming hot dirt called lava. Two good men, who were brothers, were living in Catania when the volcano poured out tons of hot lava upon the city.

The brothers saw the lava flowing right toward their parents' house. In the house were many precious things, but the two men did not give these a thought. Their first thought, instead, was for their parents, who were very old and would not be able to run to safety. One man lifted their father onto his shoulders, and the other, their mother, and they began to run.

Seeing the lava catching up to them, the parents cried, "Leave us and save yourselves!" But those two loving sons said, "Either we save you or we die with you!"

God rewarded the love of these men for their parents. When the boiling lava reached them, it divided and flowed on either side of them, without touching them at all! So both they and their parents were saved.

## In the Classroom

**Roleplaying.** Ask the children to act out some real life situations in which they have to make a choice. The same group of children might act out each scene two or three times, showing good and less perfect solutions. Some such situations would be:

A new girl comes to school.

An old man is walking down the street carrying a bag of groceries.

A baby brother is crying in his play pen.

A big sister is washing the dishes.

Dad is raking the lawn.

*Discuss:* In what different ways could a child react to these situations? Which solutions that the children act out most resemble the way Jesus Himself would have acted?

## At Home or in the Classroom

**Example of strictness being love.** Suppose your little sister asked you to let her play with a big knife that Mother uses to cut meat. Would you let her?... Suppose she kept teasing, "Please let me have it! Please! It is so bright and shiny!" Would you give in, and say, "Okay, take it"?... No, you wouldn't, no matter how hard she teased you for it. Now, sometimes what you want to do is not good for you, even though you think it would be lots of fun—just as the little sister thought it would be lots of fun to play with a bright, shiny knife. That is why your parents do not say "yes" to you, no matter how many times you ask for certain permissions. It is your own good that makes them say *no.*

Tell me, wouldn't your little sister be grateful to you, when she is older, that you did not let her have a knife to play with as a child?... She might have cut herself badly! In the same way, when you are older, you will be grateful to your parents for saying *no* to you at certain times.

Sometimes, parents even have to punish their children. But good children are grateful, because they know that their parents punish them for their own good.

# 6
# Jesus Teaches Us To Use God's Gifts Well

## TO PARENTS AND TEACHERS

The commandments treated in this lesson are the sixth and ninth, seventh and tenth. As do all the commandments, these four call for special stress in our times, when young children are exposed to so many bad examples through the electronic and print media and their contacts with boys and girls who are older or wiser in the ways of the secular world.

## PREPARATION

### Theme and Aim

God has given us gifts that we should respect and care for.
"I will take good care of all God's gifts."

### Key Words

body        food
clothes     money

### Suggested Preparatory Reading
Ephesians 5:3-5
Luke 12:15
2 Corinthians 8:12-15; 9:6-12

## Materials

pictures of (beautiful) churches

# PRESENTATION

## Introduction

*Class could be opened with the one-line prayer in the textbook (chapter 5):* "My God, for love of You, I love everybody," *followed by a review of some of the points in the activity book assignment.*

*Show the class one or more pictures of churches —beautiful ones, if possible. Talk about why church buildings are so important.* (Because God lives in churches in a special way.)

## Message

Did you ever stop and think that **we** are like churches, too? *Wait for response.* How can this be true...? *The children will probably have many good answers; guide them to the best one:* God lives in us because of Baptism. *You might turn back to lesson 2 and notice that by Baptism we became temples (churches) of the Blessed Trinity.*

Because we are like churches, we should treat our bodies with great respect. God lives in us. So we should not do anything with our bodies that our parents have told us is wrong.

We also have to be careful about what we see, hear and say.

There are bad pictures that we should not look at. *If you know where the children are likely to have seen such, be more specific.* It would not be wrong if we saw these pictures by mistake, but we should not do it on purpose.

There are television programs which are not always good. *Perhaps some children are already aware of this. You might ask them, before naming those that you have in mind. The same could be done regarding motion pictures and any other dangers you feel should be mentioned.*

There are words, stories and jokes that we sometimes call "dirty." We should not listen to them or tell them. These stories and jokes do not respect the body, which is a wonderful gift of God to us.

*Talk about the topic as long as you think you should. Knowing your locality, you will have an idea of what the children are being exposed to. Try, however, not to arouse scruples and anxiety in the more sheltered members of the class.*

*Then pass on to God's law regarding earthly goods. . . .*

God has given us other gifts besides our bodies. Can you name some? *Welcome each response. If possible, write them down in two categories: the gifts we have already talked about in connection with chapters 1—5 (such as God's grace, our family, the sun and moon . . .) and the gifts we have not mentioned yet. Circle or underline every gift in this second category that could be considered a possession.*

*Talk about what God expects of us in regard to what we and our families own. Be concrete: God expects us to feed the puppy when it is time, to try not to let the paint get scraped off our bike, to turn off the water faucet when we have as much water as we need, etc. Talk about how pleased God is when we share our things with others or give them away (with parents' permission) to those who are poorer than ourselves.*

*After discussing personal and family property, turn to the possessions of others:* is it right to take something that belongs to someone else? *Discuss.* Is it right to keep something we find? *"Decide" what should be done when we find something that someone else has lost.* Is it right to write on the walls of buildings? *Discuss.* What about breaking windows? What about writing on the desks or chairs at school?

*Cover whatever areas you think need particular attention. Also go into the duty of restitution. Explain that if you take something that belongs to someone else, you should give it back.*

*Talk about what to do when a friend tries to get us to steal or to damage something. Let the children give suggestions as to how to handle the problem.*

*Encourage them to form the habit of praying for strength from God, so that they will be able to "stand on their own feet" and not give in to the suggestions of boys or girls who want them to do something that Jesus does not like.*

God has a special love for boys and girls who try to be close to Him by being good. And when we try to be good we are happy. **God** makes us happy.

## In the Textbook

*Read the chapter carefully.*

# REINFORCEMENT

## Summary

God has given us many gifts. He has given us our bodies. We should respect them because God lives in us. He has given us many things. We should take good care of them. He has given things to other people, too. We should not take or harm what belongs to others.

## Application

"I will take good care of all God's gifts." I will respect my body and be careful about what I look at, listen to and say. I will take good care of my own things, and not take or harm what belongs to others.

## Activity

*Play some lively music. Have the children form a circle and release their energies by skipping around the room. (If possible the tune could be "God's Rules for Me"—*

*from the cassette "I Am a Child of God"—which the class will be learning next week.)*

*Then, invite the class to recite the poem "Jesus' Rule of Love," which is in the poem and song section of the activity book.*

## Assignment

*Make sure that the children understand what to do in their activity books.*

# ADDITIONAL AIDS AND ACTIVITIES

## At Home

**Charitable Project.** Repair, wash or paint an old toy and give it to the poor (through a parish organization, the St. Vincent de Paul Society, etc.).

## As a Class or Family

**Stewardship Project.** Select something in the house or classroom that needs to be mended, painted, etc., and try to make it look like new. Or undertake a litter clean-up campaign in the neighborhood, schoolyard, etc.

## At Home

**Modesty Check-up.** See whether the children are dressing as modestly as they should and, if necessary, buy some new clothes or alter the ones they have. Also check on their TV viewing habits and question them about the kind of language their friends use.

# 7
# Jesus Teaches Us To Love the Truth

## TO PARENTS AND TEACHERS

In this lesson, the children will learn something about the eighth commandment and have their first look at the commandments as a group. It is important to stress the purpose of these rules of life. God gave them to us for our own good — to protect ourselves and others and to help us live the right way, so that He can reward us with heaven.

## TO PARENTS ESPECIALLY

The formation of Christian judgments on moral issues is very important. Modern society is not God-centered; the values to which the child is exposed in school and through the communications media are often far from Christian. Therefore, it is important to help your boy or girl realize that he or she must live by God's standards, not man's. Guide your child in the formation of his conscience, helping him to understand what God's standards **are.**

## PREPARATION

### Theme and Aim

God asks us always to tell the truth. This rule and the other rules we have learned are called the ten commandments of God.

"I will be truthful always." I will keep **all** of God's commandments.

## Key Words

> truth
> commandments
> rules

## Suggested Preparatory Reading

> Ephesians 4:24-25
> Proverbs 12:19-22

## Materials

> optional—
> film "God's Rules for Me"

## PRESENTATION

### Introduction

*After a spontaneous prayer led by the teacher or by one or more children, review the preceding lesson by asking what it was about. Help the children to cover all the main points.*

### Message

*Call two boys to the front of the room (or if teaching your child at home, simply sum up the make-believe situation you are going to present).*
We are going to pretend that (1)_____ wrote on somebody's wall. (2)_____ will pretend to be (1)'s_____ father. Father, what will you say to your son? *Wait for response.* Son, what will you say to your father? *If the boy says he is sorry, etc., ask the class what some other boy*

*might have said. If they don't come up with an example of a lie, ask them whether they have ever heard someone say, "I didn't do it," when he or she really had.*

*Let the boys return to their seats and talk about lying. Ask the children to imagine how life would be if people usually told lies instead of the truth. No one could be sure of anything without seeing it firsthand.*

God loves the truth, and because we are His children He wants us to love the truth, too. All people are brothers and sisters of one another. Good brothers and sisters do not lie to one another. We should never lie to any of God's children.

## In the Textbook

*Read the chapter, including the list of the ten commandments. Explain that the commandments say everything we have been learning in class but in different words.*

*Go through the commandments one by one, pointing out their meaning:*

1 – To talk to God in prayer.

2 – To speak of God with respect.

3 – To pray to God at Mass every Sunday and Holy Day (or the night before).

4 – To love, help and obey parents.

5 – To be kind to everyone.

6 and 9 – To respect our body and be careful about what we look at, listen to or say.

7 and 10 – To take care of our things and neither take nor harm the things of others.

8 – To tell the truth always.

*Explain that God has given us these rules for our own good. When we obey them, we are happy and make others happy. We please God, too, and are on our way towards heaven.*

## REINFORCEMENT

### Summary

God asks us to always tell the truth. This is one of the rules, called the ten commandments, that He has given us.

### Application

"I will be truthful always." I will keep **all** of God's commandments.

### Activity

*Showing the film again or using the cassette, teach the song "God's Rules for Me." If you have neither film nor cassette, the song may be recited as a poem. The children will find the words in their activity books (lesson 7). The gestures are as follows:*

| | |
|---|---|
| Come with me. | *Class stands in circle. Each child beckons.* |
| Hear and see. | *Hand cupped to ear; then eyes shaded.* |
| God made rules<br>for you and me. | *Arms upward.* |
| I'll be good,<br>very good,<br>doing what<br>God says I should. | *Hands folded.* |
| I will love,<br>really love,<br>love and pray to<br>God above. | *Hands crossed on breast.* |
| I will pray<br>the right way | *1 finger held up.* |
| and God's name<br>devoutly say. | *2 fingers...* |
| Really, truly,<br>I love God | *Circle, clapping hands.* |

and He loves me!
Really, truly,
heaven's joys
I want to see!            *Stop; face center.*

Special day               *3 fingers*
God's own day —
On His day at church I'll pray.

Every day                 *4 fingers*
I'll obey,
Doing all my parents say.

I'm polite.               *5 fingers*
I don't fight.
To be kind is my delight.

I won't watch,            *6 fingers*
Do or say
Anything not right today.

    *(Repeat chorus while circling and clapping.)*
If I take,                *7 fingers*
Spoil, or break —
Much unhappiness I make.

If I lied,                *8 fingers*
I can't hide;
God sees all my thoughts inside.

I'll enjoy                *9 fingers, then ten*
Friends and toys
And not envy others' joys.

Good acts shine —         *(Arms open,*
Yours and mine —          *extended upwards)*
Shine in heaven all the time.

    *(Repeat chorus while circling and clapping.)*


## Assignment

    *Explain the brief activity book exercise and ask the children to try to memorize "God's Rules for Me."*

## ADDITIONAL AIDS AND ACTIVITIES

### In the Classroom

**Commandments game.** With felt-tip marker, letter the following numbers on stiff cards (index size or larger).

1
2
3
4
5
6 and 9
7 and 10
8

On the chalkboard or large sheets of paper, copy the simple explanations of the commandments that were in this lesson's presentation (under the section "in the textbook"), without writing the numbers.

Divide the class into two teams and have them stand in lines. They are to take turns answering when you hold up the numbered flash cards. Each time the first person in line reads off the description that matches the number, his team wins a point and he goes to the end of the line.

As soon as this game has become easy, remove the descriptions and let the children say them from memory.

### At Home or in the Classroom

**The story of Moses.** Tell this story with the amount of detail that you think will interest the children. The following undoubtedly contains more details than you will wish to relate. The point to stress is that through Moses God gave the ten commandments to all people, and that the commandments are for our own good.

At one time some people called the Israelites or Hebrews lived in a country called Egypt. The king of Egypt, called Pharaoh, hated the Israelites, so he ordered that all their baby boys be killed and thrown into the River Nile.

But God saved one little boy. He was a beautiful baby, and his mother and father hid him for three months so that he would not be killed. When they could hide him no longer, they put him into a little basket and placed it in the weeds near the

Nile River bank. His sister stood on the bank of the river, watching the little basket hidden away in the weeds. The king's daughter came down to the river and saw the little basket. When she opened it, how surprised she was to see a little baby! She loved him so much that she decided to keep him.

She named the little baby Moses.

One day when Moses was a grown-up man, he was out in the desert taking care of the sheep. Suddenly, he saw a bush on fire.

As Moses looked on, he saw that the bush, though on fire, did not burn up. So he decided, "I must go over to look at this wonderful sight and see why the bush is not burned." But **God** called out to him from the bush, "Moses! Moses!"

Moses answered, "Here I am."

God said, "Come no nearer! Remove the sandals from your feet, for the place where you stand is holy ground. I am the God of your father," He continued, "the God of Abraham, the God of Isaac, the God of Jacob."

Moses hid his face, for he was afraid to look at God. Then the Lord said, "I have seen the suffering of my people in Egypt.... Therefore, I have come down to rescue them from the hands of the Egyptians and lead them out of that land into a good and spacious land, a land flowing with milk and honey.... Come now! I will send you to Pharaoh to lead my people, the Israelites, out of Egypt."

The Lord then gave Moses the gift of miracles: "Take the rod you have in your hand and throw it on the ground," He said. Moses obeyed. The rod immediately changed into a snake, and Moses drew away from it. "Take hold of its tail," the Lord said. Moses put out his hand, and laid hold of it, and it became a rod again.

"You will work these miracles that they may believe that it is I who have sent you," said God.

After that, Moses and his brother Aaron went to Pharaoh and said, "Thus says the Lord, the God of Israel: Let my people go, so that they may celebrate a feast to me in the desert."

Proudly Pharaoh answered, "Who is the Lord, that I should hear His plea to let Israel go? I do not know the Lord; even if I did, I would not let Israel go."

To convince him, Moses worked many miracles in his presence, but, blinded by pride, Pharaoh would not give in. In fact, he ordered that the Hebrews be treated more cruelly than before. To force Pharaoh to let His people go, the Lord then sent ten terrible punishments, called the **ten plagues of Egypt.** He said to Moses:

"Pharaoh's heart is stubborn in refusing to let the people go. Tomorrow morning, when he goes toward the river, present yourself before him on the bank of the Nile, holding in your hand the staff that changed into a serpent. Say to Pharaoh: 'The Lord, the God of the Hebrews, sent me to you with the message: Let my people go to worship me in the desert. But you have still not listened. The Lord now says: This is how you shall know I am the Lord. I will strike the water of the Nile with the staff that is in my hand, and it shall turn into blood. The fish in the Nile will die, and the river itself shall become so polluted that the Egyptians will be unable to drink its water."

Moses and Aaron carried out God's command, and the water in rivers, streams, pools, wells and water jars became bloody.

This was the first plague.

But Pharaoh did not give in.

A second plague came. The Nile became filled with frogs, which came swarming up its banks to invade the land – streets, public squares, homes and even beds!

The third plague occurred when Aaron struck the dust of the earth, which turned into great swarms of winged insects that made life miserable for both men and animals.

Then there were the flies that infested everything. This was followed by the death of many of the horses, cattle, camels, donkeys and sheep of the Egyptians. This was the fifth plague.

Then Moses took two handfuls of soot from a furnace and flung it into the air. The dust blew far and wide, causing painful boils to rise on the skin of men and the hides of beasts. But Pharaoh did not give in, even in the face of this sixth plague. Then the sky filled with clouds; there were great peals of thunder and flashes of lightning, and a fierce hail poured down upon the land – the seventh plague.

This was followed by an invasion of locusts, which devoured everything that remained after the hail storm. This was the eighth plague, and Pharaoh was really shaken by it. As he had done a few times before, he promised to let the people go, but then as soon as the danger had passed he took back his promise.

Then a great darkness fell over the land of Egypt for three days. After it had gone, Moses and Aaron went to have a discussion with Pharaoh. But Pharaoh still refused to let the Israelites go.

The reason Pharaoh was so stubborn was that the Egyptians were accustomed to seeing some of these things happen. Every year, at the beginning of the spring floods, the Nile turned red because of the great quantities of volcanic ash picked up by the high waters; at other times, frogs swarmed up the river-banks and overran the countryside; so, too, the scorching winds from the nearby desert often picked up so much sand in the springtime as to blot out the light of the sun.

But this time it was God who brought about these disturbing things. These were true miracles worked by Him; in fact, they took place one after another and when Moses gave the signal, rather than at different seasons, and only the Egyptians were bothered by them, while the Israelites were not.

In God's name, Moses and Aaron threatened Pharaoh with the tenth plague, the worst of all: the death of all the first-born children of the Egyptians. Pharaoh still stubbornly refused to let the Hebrews go.

God ordered Moses and Aaron to prepare the people to flee out of Egypt.

"Tell the whole community of Israel," God said to Moses, "that every family must obtain for itself a lamb without any spot or defect, and then kill it during the evening twilight. They shall take some of its blood and apply it to the two doorposts and to the lintel of the house. That same night they shall eat its roasted flesh with unleavened bread and bitter herbs. They must eat it with sandals on their feet and their staffs in their hands, like those who are in flight. For I will go through Egypt and strike down every first-born of the land except in the houses where there is the blood of the lamb."

All the Israelite families did as Moses commanded.

And then an angel of death killed all the first-born sons of the Egyptians, including the son of Pharaoh. But the angel passed over every home which had the lamb's blood on its door posts. For that reason, the lamb — called the paschal lamb — whose blood saved the Hebrews is now seen to be a type or symbol of Christ, the Lamb of God, whose death saved us all from slavery to sin.

Hearing the loud wailing of the Egyptians who had lost their children, the Pharaoh called Moses and Aaron. He ordered them to leave with all the Israelites at once to offer sacrifice to the Lord in the desert.

Thus, after many years in Egypt, the Hebrew people left for the Promised Land. This journey is called the Exodus. It is also called the Passover, from which comes our English word **paschal,** referring to the celebration of the Jewish Passover and the Christian Easter.

"This day," the Lord had told the Israelites, "shall be a memorial feast for you, which all your generations shall celebrate with lasting ceremony."

And indeed, in the desert and in the Promised Land of Canaan the Israelites would never forget to celebrate the Passover feast. It became the duty of the youngest son in the family to ask his father the reason for the ceremony. Every year the father would repeat the same explanation: "This is the Passover sacrifice of the Lord, who, when we were slaves of the Egyptians, passed over the houses of the Israelites while He struck down the Egyptians. He set us free...."

The Israelites soon found a large body of water before them. It was then called the Sea of Reeds, and was located near one of the arms of the Red Sea. God, who is all-powerful, saw to it that His people passed through this sea miraculously. He sent a strong, hot wind from the east, which blew for several hours and drove the waters off a shallow crossing place. The Israelites crossed on dry land. Then God let the wind stop, and the waters flowed back to their usual position. These waters caught the Egyptians, who had changed their minds and were chasing the Israelites. The Bible recounts the miracle in words similar to these:

Then Moses stretched out his hand over the sea, and the Lord swept the sea with a strong east wind all night long and so turned it into dry land. When the water was thus divided, the Israelites marched into the midst of the sea on dry land, with the water like a wall to their right and to their left. The Egyptians followed in pursuit; all Pharaoh's horses and chariots and charioteers went after them right into the midst of the sea.... Then the Lord told Moses: "Stretch out your hand over the sea, that the water may flow back upon the Egyptians, upon their chariots and charioteers." So Moses stretched out his hand over the sea, and at dawn the sea flowed back to its normal depth. As the water flowed back, it covered the chariots and charioteers of Pharaoh's whole army which had followed the Israelites into the sea.

The passage through the Red Sea is a symbol or type of Baptism, by which we are freed from the slavery to sin, as the Hebrews were freed from their slavery to Pharaoh.

From the Red Sea the Hebrews began to travel through the desert of the Sinai peninsula. God went ahead of them as a bright cloud by day and a fiery cloud by night. But the Israelites began to complain. When their food ran out in the desert, they began to long for the meat and tasty food they had had in Egypt.

Moses then told them, "The Lord will give you meat to eat this evening and tomorrow He will give you your fill of bread."

In the evening a flock of tasty birds called quail appeared and covered the camp. The Hebrews took them and ate their fill.

In the morning, when they arose, they found fine white flakes on the ground. They went about asking each other: "Manu?" — which in their language meant: "What is this?" Thus the food was called **manna**. The manna fell every morning, except on Saturday, which was the Lord's special day. It tasted like wafers made with honey. Everyone was to gather enough manna for the day, and on the day before Saturday all gathered a double amount.

The manna came down six days a week, year in and year out, for forty years, until the Israelites entered the Promised Land.

Manna was a symbol of the Holy Eucharist, the true Bread of heaven, which sustains us in the desert of life.

When the water supply ran out, Moses struck a rock in the presence of the people, by command of God, and at once a great supply of fresh water gushed forth to satisfy the Hebrews' thirst.

Should we envy the Israelites because of all the things God did for them in the desert? Not at all! God lovingly provides for our **spiritual** needs in an even more marvelous manner. He sent His own Son, our Lord Jesus Christ, to save us. Jesus Christ lives in our midst, in the Blessed Sacrament of the altar. He is the food of our souls in Holy Communion. He forgives our sins in confession. God has given each of us a guardian angel, too. The Lord gives to all men the graces they need to save their souls. (If they are not saved, it is their own fault.)

So we can see that God does even more wonderful things for us than He did for the Israelites years ago.

In the third month after their departure from Egypt, the Hebrews reached the foot of Mount Sinai.

Moses went up the mountain and received from God the following order: "On the third day the Lord will come down on Mount Sinai before the eyes of all the people. Set limits for the people all around the mountain and tell them: Take care not to go up the mountain, or even to touch its base."

On the morning of the third day there were bursts of thunder and lightning, and a heavy cloud over the mountain, and a very loud trumpet blast, so that all the people in the camp shook with fear.

Moses led the people out of the camp to meet God. Fearfully, they waited at the foot of the mountain. Alone, Moses went up. Then from the top of the mountain, God said:

"I, the Lord, am your God.

"You shall not have other gods besides me, nor shall you worship them. For I, the Lord your God, am a jealous God, punishing those who hate me, but showing mercy to those who love me and keep my commandments.

"You shall not take the name of the Lord, your God, in vain.

"Remember to keep holy the Sabbath Day. Six days you may labor, but on the seventh, no work may be done.

"Honor your father and your mother, that you may have a long life.

"You shall not kill.

"You shall not commit impure acts.

"You shall not steal.

"You shall not bear false witness against your neighbor.

"You shall not covet your neighbor's wife.

"You shall not covet your neighbor's house or any other thing that belongs to him."

All the people solemnly promised to obey these ten commandments of the Lord. "We will do everything that the Lord has told us!" they exclaimed.

God gave these very same commandments to us, too, for we are the New People of God. It is our duty to know and practice them. By keeping the ten commandments, we show our love of God and neighbor and live a good and happy life.

# 8
# Sin Leads People
# Away from God

## TO PARENTS AND TEACHERS

In a sin-saturated society, this may be a difficult topic to teach about. It certainly cannot be presented as something uncommon. But the essence of sin lies in God's displeasure, not in a breach of human customs. Sin is a breaking of God's law, an offense to Him, a turning of the will away from Him. In teaching sin's relationship to God, however, we must not lose sight of another fact: sin harms ourselves and others.

## TO PARENTS ESPECIALLY

If at all possible, your child should have the example of parents who regularly experience reconciliation with God and His people in the sacrament of Penance. It would be well for you to receive this sacrament during these weeks of your child's preparation, lest sooner or later he wonder whether confession is only for children. He could accompany you to church and receive his first instruction about Penance in a very informal way by observing how his parents and other members of the parish community approach the sacrament of God's mercy.

## PREPARATION

### Theme and Aim

Sin is disobedience to God. It displeases God and harms ourselves and others.

"I will ask God's forgiveness."

### Key Words

disobedience
sin
Church

### Suggested Preparatory Reading

The Book of Jonah

### Materials

optional —

flannelboard figures for the parable of Jonah

## PRESENTATION

### Introduction

The opening prayer could be followed by the singing (or recitation) of "God's Rules for Me" (lesson 7 — activity book). Then discuss the meaning of the song, line by line.

Ask the children whether they know when God's rules were given to people. If the children had a chance to learn about Moses last week, they may be able to tell something about the giving of the commandments on Mt. Sinai.

Now, emphasize Jesus' attitude toward the ten commandments. He said that He had come to make them even more perfect (see Matthew 5:17-18).

This shows us that the ten commandments are very, very important.

## Message

Do you know what we call it when a person breaks one of God's rules — in other words, disobeys one of God's commandments? *See whether the children are familiar with the word "sin."*

I would like to tell you a story from God's Holy Book, the Bible. This story will explain something about sin.

*The story is the parable of Jonah. You may use flannelboard figures if available. Be careful to stress these two points: (1) sin displeases God; (2) God loves everyone and forgives people who are sorry.*

Part of this story is only a story, but the rest of it is very important. That is why God wanted it written down in His Holy Book, the Bible.

This is the story:

Long ago there lived a man named Jonah. God called Jonah to be His special messenger. "Go to the big city of Nineveh," God told Jonah. "People there are committing many sins. Go tell them so."

But Jonah did not want to go to Nineveh. He was thinking something like this: "If I tell those people how displeased God is, they might become sorry for their sins. If they become sorry, God will forgive them. I don't want that to happen, because I don't like the people of Nineveh."

So, instead of going toward Nineveh, Jonah went off in a different direction. In fact, he got on a boat that was going to a different country!

But when the boat was on the sea a big storm came up. The wind grew so strong that soon the waves were taller than the boat. It seemed as if the boat would sink.

"Whose fault is this?" the sailors asked one another. Then they turned to Jonah and asked him, "Who are you? Where are you going and why?"

Jonah told them that he was running away from God and from what God had told him to do.

"How could you do such a thing?" the sailors asked. "And what can we do now to make the storm stop?"

"Throw me into the sea," said Jonah.

The men didn't want to do that, but finally, they did. And as soon as they had thrown Jonah into the sea, the storm calmed down.

There was Jonah in the sea! What would happen to him? What do you think? Well, a very big fish came along and swallowed him!

Jonah was still alive inside the fish. He stayed there for three days and three nights. And while he was inside the fish, he said a prayer to God. He told God that he trusted Him.

God answered Jonah's prayer. After three days and three nights the big fish swam to the shore and threw Jonah up onto the beach.

Now we are coming to the really important part of our story. Again God told Jonah, "Go to Nineveh and give the people the message I will tell you."

This time, Jonah **did** go to Nineveh. And he walked all through the city, shouting, "In forty days, God will destroy this city because of the sins of its people!"

This message is like many others that we find in God's Book, the Bible. Sin displeases God very much. Over and over again the Bible tells us that God hates sin. You remember what sin is—disobedience to God.

The people of Nineveh listened to Jonah and became frightened. In fact, the king said, "Let us go without eating or drinking, and let us tell God that we are sorry. Who knows—maybe He will forgive us and not destroy our city!"

And that was exactly what happened! Because the people of Nineveh became sorry and tried to make up for their sins, God forgave them.

This is another important lesson that we find in the story of Jonah and other parts of the Bible. God loves all people, even though they commit sins, and when they are sorry and try to be good, He forgives them. God is that way with each one of us, because He loves us all.

## In the Textbook

Read the lesson. The list of questions (you might point out) is a list of good things. Their opposites (as listed in chapter 12, for example) would be sins.

Optional — More Details

Who can tell me the name of the sin that every baby is born with?... Yes, that is right. We were all born with **original sin.**

Original sin was removed at Baptism. After Baptism, a soul is spotless, very beautiful and pleasing to God. It is bright with God's wonderful life.

How long does the soul stay bright and beautiful? As long as the person does not offend God with personal sin. Personal, or actual, sins are the sins that we ourselves commit.

Suppose one of you did something wrong without knowing that it was wrong. Would you commit a sin? No, you would not, because you did not know it was a sin. To commit sin, the person must know he or she is doing something wrong. What if a boy accidentally bumps his sister so hard that she falls and breaks her arm? Would he have committed a sin? No, because he did not mean to hurt his sister. It was an accident, not a sin. To commit a sin, a person must **intend** to do something he knows is wrong.

*At this point, you may wish to give more examples to bring out clearly the difference between sins and inadvertent or accidental misdemeanors. Your pupils rarely if ever do evil knowingly and deliberately; their faults are generally the result of their impulsiveness and lack of knowledge. Hence, it is important that while they are taught the evil of breaking God's laws, they also be taught that the sin must be known and willed. It is well to give examples drawn from the children's daily lives, examples of the faults into which they most easily fall, such as quarreling, lying, becoming jealous, disobeying, etc.*

Sin is committed in five different ways: 1) in **thoughts**; 2) in **desires**; 3) in **words**; 4) in **actions**; and 5) in **omissions.**

Some children think that no one sees their thoughts, so they can think what they please. Is that right? No. God sees all our thoughts, and it is wrong to keep bad thoughts in our mind.

Jimmy's mother has told him that he must stay home to help his daddy clean up the yard. Jimmy wants to go play with his friends. He thinks: "My mother is mean! I'm mad at her. I don't like her at all!" Is it all right for Jimmy to keep these thoughts in mind? No! He is committing a sin of **thought.**

Mary Lou has a friend who was not a very nice little girl. She is always trying to get Mary Lou to do things her mother has told her not to do. One day Mary Lou's mother told her that she could not play with her friend anymore. Mary Lou went up to her bedroom saying to herself: "I wish my mother would go shopping so that I could sneak over to my friend's house. I want to do the things Mother doesn't want me to do." Were Mary Lou's **desires** good?

Once I heard two boys calling one another names. How they were yelling at each other! It was terrible! They were both as angry as they could be, and they were saying terrible things. They were committing sins of **word.**

Sins of **action** are all such bad actions as stealing, disobeying, fighting, reading bad books, etc.

What are sins of omission? "Omission" means not doing something we are supposed to do. When a person sins by omission, he does not do something he should have done. For example, suppose Bobby knows that he is supposed to go to school today, but he feels like playing. So he skips school. Bobby has done wrong because he has not gone to school as he should have. Margaret skips Mass on Sunday just because she doesn't feel like going. These are sins of **omission.**

Some sins are worse than others. They are called **mortal** sins. They drive God's life out of a person's soul.

A sin is mortal when 1) the sin is big, 2) we know that it is something big before we do it, 3) we decide to do it anyway.

**Venial** sin is not as bad as mortal sin. It does not rob our souls of God's life. But venial sin **does** displease God. It offends Him and it hurts ourselves and others. It is the next worst evil in the world — after mortal sin. And venial sin weakens God's life in us, too.

A sin is venial 1) when the sin is small; 2) when the sin is big but the person believes it is small; 3) when the sin is big, but the person does not really want to do it.

The saints tried to avoid even the tiniest faults. And when they did slip into some fault, they were very, very sad to think that they had offended Jesus.

Whenever St. Therese of the Child Jesus was told that something she was doing displeased Jesus, she would stop it at once. Nor would she ever do it again. She was still just a little child then, but already she loved Jesus very much. Each night when her mother tucked her in bed, she would ask her:

"Is Jesus pleased with me for the way I acted today?"

The answer was always, "yes."

I hope **your** mothers will always be able to say the same to you!

Let us say the last part of the Our Father to ask God to keep us free from sin:

Give us this day . . . .

## REINFORCEMENT

### Summary

Sin is disobedience to God and His rules. Sin displeases God, hurts the person who does it, and hurts God's "family," the Church.

### Application

"I will ask God's forgiveness" and I will try very hard not to commit sins.

### Activity

Invite the class to sing "God's Rules for Me" with its accompanying gestures.

## Assignment

*Show the children how to do the activity book home-work for lesson 8.*

# ADDITIONAL AIDS AND ACTIVITIES

## At Home or in the Classroom

Invite the children (individually or as a group) to make a comic strip of the story of Jonah. First reread or retell it. Give them pre-punched sheets of drawing paper, which can be tied together in booklet form.

## In the Classroom

Dramatize the story of Jonah, as recounted in this manual. The teacher could jot down each child's lines and the cue for each and give them a few minutes to memorize or paraphrase them. "God" will speak from off-stage. A table may serve as the ship; the area under a desk as the interior of the fish; the aisles of the class-room as the streets of Nineveh. The cast consists of:

Narrator — the teacher, who rereads the story, except for the spoken lines

God — who does not appear but speaks, if possible, from outside the room

Jonah

3 sailors

the king of Nineveh

The remaining members of the class can represent the people of Nineveh. Their role will be to listen to Jonah as he walks up and down. When the teacher reads: "Be-cause the people of Nineveh became sorry..." the children clasp their hands in prayer, some bowing their heads, others looking up to heaven.

# 9
# Jesus Is
# Our Savior

## TO PARENTS AND TEACHERS

In this lesson the children become more aware of God's loving forgiveness. Displeasing as sin is to Him, our heavenly Father is always ready to pardon the sinner who is sorry. His ways are not ours (cf. Isaiah 55:6-9); He holds no grudges. God is mercy. God is love.

If we ourselves have experienced this consoling truth, we will be better able to help the children to grasp it.

## PREPARATION

### Theme and Aim

Jesus died because He wanted to save us — to free us from sin. I will remember often that Jesus saved me by dying on the cross.

### Key Words

cross
suffered
died
rose

## Suggested Preparatory Reading

Luke 15:3-7
John 10:9-18
Luke 23:33-49
John 19:28-30

## Materials

optional —
large picture of sheep and a shepherd
filmstrip "My Friend Jesus"
pictures of some or all of the stations of the cross
crucifix or picture of the crucifixion
statue of the Sacred Heart

# PRESENTATION

## Introduction

Say the "Our Father" and review the meaning of: "Lead us not into temptation, but deliver us from evil." Go over the activity book assignment by asking questions based on it.

## Message

Ask the children to think of a big crowd of people and a family trying to make its way through the crowd. If possible, give an example of a park or other recreation site that the children are familiar with. The father tells the children to make sure that they stay together, but one of the younger children sees something interesting and goes off in another direction....

Discuss: Was it right or wrong for this boy (or girl) to do this? What could happen? Why did the parents tell him (her) to stay with the others?

What would happen when that father in the park realized his little boy (or girl) was missing?

Wait for response.

Yes, he would go to find him (or her). And that's what Jesus does when people disobey His heavenly Father and run away from Him by committing sin. Jesus goes to look for them. In fact, Jesus called Himself the **Good Shepherd.** I will tell you a story which shows what this means.

*Pin up a picture of sheep and shepherd, if you have one. Explain "sheep," "lamb," "flock," "shepherd" and "sheepfold" before beginning the story.*

Once there was a shepherd who had a hundred sheep. Each day he would take them out of the sheepfold and walk with them out to the green pastures, where there was much grass for the sheep to eat. The shepherd and his sheep would spend the whole day out in the fields. Then at night the shepherd would bring all the sheep back to the sheepfold, where they would be safe until morning.

One evening when the shepherd counted his sheep he found only ninety-nine instead of a hundred. One of the sheep was missing! So the shepherd, who was a very good shepherd, left the ninety-nine together, with his dog to take care of them, and went to look for the one that was missing.

On and on the shepherd walked, up hills and down valleys. He kept calling for the lost sheep, because when sheep hear their shepherd's voice they come to him. But no sheep came.

Meanwhile, the lost sheep was caught in a bush full of thorns. The thorns were digging into his wool so that he couldn't move. The sheep was frightened, because he was only a little lamb. He had never been away from the flock before. He had always been told never to leave the flock. And now he was so sorry that he had disobeyed!

Suddenly the little lamb saw two eyes shining in the darkness. He heard a stick break. Something was coming toward him! Was it a wolf? Was it a wildcat? The little lamb wanted to run. But he couldn't. He was caught in the thorn bush.

Then the lamb heard the good shepherd calling to him. "Baaaa!" cried out the lamb. He called as loud as he could: "Baaaa!"

The shepherd was coming – the lamb could hear him. The animal with the bright eyes heard the shepherd, too.

It ran away, making crackling and rustling noises in the bushes.

"Baaaa," called the lamb again.

"There you are!" said the good shepherd. The lamb could see him against the sky. The shepherd bent over. He could hardly see the lamb in the darkness. He began to untangle the lamb from the thorn bush. But because he couldn't see well, he kept getting pricked by the sharp thorns. But he didn't mind getting hurt. He was only worried about the lamb, not about himself.

At last the lamb was free from the bush! The good shepherd picked him up. He put him across his shoulders so he could carry him more easily. Then he started for home.

How happy the lamb was now! He was very sorry that he had disobeyed but very glad that the good shepherd had come such a long way to find him and save him from the wild animals.

(pause)

Jesus is like that good shepherd. In fact, He **called** Himself the Good Shepherd. And do you know what He said about the Good Shepherd? The Good Shepherd **dies** for His sheep. That's what Jesus did. He **died** for us.

Maybe you know something about Jesus' death already. But let me tell you again, because this is very important....

Alternate Options—

1—Show the remainder of the filmstrip "My Friend Jesus," which the class began to view a few weeks ago.

2—*If possible, prominently display a crucifix or a picture of the crucifixion. Then tell the story:*

Many, many people loved Jesus, because He was so good. People who couldn't see, people who couldn't hear, people who couldn't walk all asked Jesus to cure them and He did. He helped everyone. So the crowds followed Him wherever He went. But there was a group of wicked men who were jealous of our Lord. They were angry because the people loved Him so much. These wicked men had Jesus arrested and condemned to death.

Jesus is God. If He had not let them, those bad men could not have hurt Him in any way. But Jesus wanted to suffer for our sins. So He let Himself be cruelly beaten with whips and crowned with sharp thorns. He let soldiers spit on Him and make fun of Him.

After being condemned to death, Jesus was given a big, heavy cross to carry up a hill called Calvary. *It might be effective to show pictures of the stations of the cross. You may wish to mention our Lord's meeting with His Sorrowful Mother, His three falls, etc.*

At the top of Calvary hill, the big cross was laid down on the ground and Jesus let the soldiers nail Him to it. They drove big nails right through His hands and right through His feet! The long, sharp thorns dug into His head. How much Jesus suffered to make up for your sins and mine! How much He loves **me,** each one of us can say.

The soldiers stood the cross up on the top of Calvary, and for three hours Jesus hung there with the nails in His bleeding hands and feet. In those three hours Jesus suffered terribly. What a dreadful thing sin is, children! See how Jesus suffered to make up for it!

After three hours of pain, Jesus died on the cross. What a great proof of His love He gave us!

Near the cross on which Jesus died stood the Blessed Mother and the apostle John. After Jesus died, the apostles took Him down and wrapped Him in a linen sheet. Then they carried Him to a tomb. The Blessed Mother walked behind them. Her heart was broken—they had killed her dear Son Jesus! *Make the scene come to life before their eyes—arouse sentiments of sorrow.*

Let us stand and thank Jesus for dying to save us from sin. We shall join our hands and bow our heads. Then each of us will pray in our heart, thanking Jesus.

*A minute of silence.*

*The concept of "satisfying for sin" may be difficult for the children to understand. It would be well to write it on the board and explain it by examples, such as the following.* Suppose your little brother broke a clock and your mother was going to spank him. Now suppose you begged her to punish you instead because you felt sorry for your little brother. You would be **satisfying** for what your brother did. That is what it means to **satisfy**.

This example gives us some idea of what Jesus did for us. He came down on earth, and lived a life of hard work and suffering, and died on the cross to save us. In that way, He **satisfied** for our sins, so that we could go to heaven.

See what an evil thing sin is! How much Jesus suffered because of sin. Let us promise to avoid sin always and to love Jesus with all our hearts.

## In the Textbook

*Read the lesson and review the meaning of the sign of the cross.*

## REINFORCEMENT

## Summary

Jesus is the Good Shepherd. He died for us, His sheep, who run away by committing sin. Jesus saved us by dying on the cross and rising from the dead.

## Application

"I will make the sign of the cross well."

## Activity

*Hold a catechetical celebration with a Good Shepherd theme:*

*If possible, arrange the children's chairs and your own in a semicircle about a desk or table bearing a statue of the Sacred Heart.*
*All stand.*

*Opening song: the chorus of "God's Rules for Me." Let the children skip as usual while singing, so that they will be less restless and more attentive during the celebration.*
*All sit.*
*Teacher:*

God is our Father. He always loves us. And He wants us to love Him, too. Sometimes we turn away from God by failing to love Him or other people. But God is always ready to take us back. Let us listen to what Jesus tells us in the story of the Good Shepherd.

*All stand.*

*The Gospel reading may be taken directly from Luke 15:1-7, or the following paraphrase may be used:*

Jesus asked the people: "If one of you has a hundred sheep and loses one, doesn't he leave the ninety-nine and follow the lost one until he finds it? And when he finds it, he is happy. He picks it up and carries it home on his shoulders. Then when he gets back he calls his friends and neighbors and tells them, 'Celebrate with me, because I have found my lost sheep.' I tell you that in just the same way there will be great joy in heaven over a sinner who is sorry."

This is the Gospel of the Lord.

*All:*

Praise to you, Lord Jesus Christ.

*All sit.*
*Teacher:*

Jesus is the Good Shepherd. He came into the world to look for us sinners and to bring us to His Father. He came to teach the way to heaven: love for God and others. But maybe we don't always love God and others the way we should. Then we are like the little lost lamb.

Now we are going to think about whether we have been good children of our heavenly Father. In order to think about ourselves, we have to sit very still without moving....

*Set the example of immobility. Softly call to any of the children who are moving. Make them notice the sounds that can still be heard inside the room — the rustling of paper, the shuffling of feet, etc. When the children are at last truly quiet, continue softly:*

Today, or maybe yesterday, did I do something that I wish I hadn't done? *Pause.* Maybe after I did it, I had an uncomfortable feeling inside. *Pause.* What was this wrong thing that I did? *Pause.* Have I done it other times? *Pause. Similar general questions may be added.*

*Note that it is best not to be specific at this point. If we suggest certain faults only, and neglect to mention a child's own particular failing, the youngster may conclude that the only real offenses against God and others are those that the teacher has mentioned or those that his parents point out to him. Detailed lists do have their place, but they must be used with discretion.*

*Continue....*

Maybe there is one thing I have done that seems especially wrong, or maybe there is some fault that I commit very often. *Pause.* It would be good for me to try to make up for this.... What could I do? *Pause.*

Now that we have thought of our faults and have planned to try to make up for them, let us ask God to forgive us. Let's bow our heads to show Him that we are sorry....

*Teacher or Helper:*

Repeat after me: Lord, have mercy.

*All:*

Lord, have mercy.

*Teacher or Helper:*

Christ, have mercy.

*All:*

Christ, have mercy.

*Teacher or Helper:*

Lord, have mercy.

*All:*

Lord, have mercy.

*Teacher:*

We know that God still loves us and that He is pleased because we are sorry. We know that He forgives us and that soon we will receive His forgiveness and help in a special way in confession. *Print the words, "Thank You, God!" on the chalkboard.* Let's say them all together.

*All:*

Thank You, God!

## Assignment

*Explain to the children what they should do in their activity books.*

## ADDITIONAL AIDS AND ACTIVITIES

### At Home or in the Classroom

**"Filmstrip" or "TV Program."** The class might be divided into groups to illustrate the parable of the Good Shepherd. They may draw on a roll of shelf paper or on uniform sheets that will be taped together. The roll of pictures may be pulled horizontally through two slits in a box that has been made to look like a TV set.

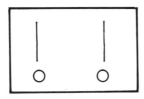

# 10
# God Always Forgives

## TO PARENTS AND TEACHERS

God's loving forgiveness—so well depicted in the parable of the Good Shepherd—is shown again in the story of the prodigal son. The former stresses God's role; the latter, our own. Familiarity with the steps the prodigal son took in returning to his father will help the children learn how to prepare to return to their heavenly Father through the sacrament of Penance.

## PREPARATION

### Theme and Aim

When we sin, we run away from God. To be happy and peaceful again, we must return to Him. "I will try to be better."

### Key Words

prodigal
forgiveness

### Suggested Preparatory Reading

Luke 15:11-32

# PRESENTATION

## Introduction

*After a spontaneous opening prayer, invite one or more children to tell the parable of the Good Shepherd. Invite other children to explain the way that Jesus is truly the Good Shepherd.*

*It might be well to go over the activity book homework in class.*

## Message

*Ask this question:*

Suppose you asked your father for some money and he gave it to you. Would your father be pleased if you took that money and dropped it into (make an appropriate local comparison—a grate in a sidewalk, a manhole, a river, the harbor...)?

*Discuss. For what good purposes could the children have used the money?*

*Show—if possible—a filmstrip on the prodigal son, such as "The Prodigal Son Returns" from the Show'n' Tell Canon Bible Series.*

*If no audiovisual is available, tell the story yourself, using any visual aids you can obtain.*

Jesus once told a story about a young man who wasted money by spending it in ways that were very bad. Later the young man was sorry. This is the story:

There was a farm owner who had two sons. The older son was a very hard worker on his father's farm. The younger son was not such a hard worker. One day the younger son asked his father for some money. The father gave it to him. A few days after that, the younger son packed up his clothes and left home. He went to another country. He began to spend his time with bad people and to live in a bad way. And he kept spending the money that his father had given him.

At last the young man's money ran out. It was all gone. When the money was gone, all the bad friends went away. Suddenly the young man was alone. He didn't have a place to live any more. He didn't even have anything to eat. There was a shortage of food, so when he asked people to give him even just a piece of bread, they would say "no."

"I'll get a job," thought the young man. But it wasn't easy to find a job. He had to look a long time before he found one.

At last he met a rich man who owned a farm. "Yes, I'll hire you," said the rich man. "You can take care of my pigs."

But the young man had to work for almost nothing. He only had a place to sleep at night and a little food. He got so hungry that he wanted to eat the corn husks—if possible, show some or a picture of them—that were given to the pigs, but nobody noticed how hungry he was. Nobody gave him anything more to eat.

"This isn't like my father's farm," thought the young man. "Why, on my father's farm, all the workers have more than enough to eat! And here I am, starving!"

The young man thought for a while. "I'd like to work for my father," he thought. "I know I shouldn't have wasted the money he gave me. I know I don't deserve to be treated like his son any more. But my father is so good that I'm sure he'll let me be a worker on his farm. I would be happy with that."

So the younger son started home. It was a long, long walk. Finally one day he saw his father's house. And then he saw his father coming to meet him! In fact, his father was running. His father had been watching for him.

The father welcomed his son with a big hug and kiss. Then the young man said, "Father, I have sinned against God and against you I don't deserve to be called your son any more."

But the father called to his servants and told them to bring his son new clothes and to prepare a big dinner. They were going to have a party! "My son has been lost, and now he has been found," the father said. He was so happy to have the young man back home. He was happy, too, that his son was sorry for what he had done wrong! He forgave his son completely!

Jesus acts just the same way with us. When we come to Him in confession and tell Him through the priest that we are sorry for the wrong we have done and that we will try to be better, Jesus and His Father forgive us and welcome us. They are so pleased with a person who wants to be forgiven and to become better! God's family is pleased, too. So when we make a good confession, God is happy, we are happy, and all God's baptized children are happy, too.

## In the Textbook

*While reading the lesson, you might wish to tell the children the name of this story: the prodigal son. They will hear this name very often. You could show them the word* **prodigal** *and explain that it means wasteful. It was a sin for the young man to waste the money, but worse yet, he used that money to commit many other sins.*

## Learning a Prayer of Sorrow

Choose an act of contrition (see activity book, chapter 12) which the children can say together in Penance celebrations. Explain the difficult words and encourage them to memorize the prayer.

## REINFORCEMENT

### Summary

When we commit sin we turn away from God, our good Father, the way the runaway young man did. To be happy and peaceful again, we must return to God.

### Application

"I will try to be better."

## Assignment

*The activity book assignment will require some explanation.*

## ADDITIONAL AIDS AND ACTIVITIES

### At Home or in the Classroom

**Drawing.** Each pupil could divide his paper in half and show—in one section—the prodigal son being welcomed by his father. In the other section the child may draw himself going to confession.

### At Home or in the Classroom

**Mural.** The children might depict the story of the prodigal son in about five scenes. Colored chalk dipped in water is a good medium.

# 11
# Jesus Brings Us the Father's Forgiveness

## TO PARENTS AND TEACHERS

In this lesson the children will begin to learn about confession itself. They should be encouraged to regard their approaching first confession as neither a final goal nor a simple stepping-stone to first Communion. Rather, may it be considered the first of many encounters with the Lord. Devotional confessions are of great value in the spiritual life, especially in a world where sin is rampant. The Church teaches that by the practice of frequent confession "genuine self-knowledge is increased, Christian humility grows, bad habits are corrected, spiritual neglect and tepidity are resisted, the conscience is purified, the will is strengthened, a salutary self-control is attained, and grace is increased" *(Mystici Corporis Christi).* Confession of slight faults is a preventative against sinful habits.

## TO PARENTS ESPECIALLY

As has been pointed out, your child will benefit greatly from the habit of frequent confession. But how is he to form this habit, unless he sees adults (whose sins, he realizes, must be "bigger" than his own) approaching the confessional or reconciliation room often?

The Church asks us to receive the sacrament of Penance "regularly." What should this mean for you and for your child? In the past many Catholics went to confession once a month and some even more often. Such frequency enables one to better remember his sins. It also fortifies the spirit against temptation and a tendency toward lukewarmness. Your child's first confession would be an excellent occasion for you to begin or renew this practice.

# PREPARATION

## Theme and Aim

In confession we tell our sins to the priest and Jesus forgives us through the priest.
"I will go to confession well."

## Key Words

sacrament
Penance (and penance)
confession
absolution and absolve

## Suggested Preparatory Reading

John 20:19-23

**FROM THE BASIC TEACHINGS FOR CATHOLIC RELIGIOUS EDUCATION:**

"Sacramental absolution, which follows upon sincere confession of sin, true sorrow, and resolution not to sin again, is a means of obtaining pardon from God. Usually given to the individual, it brings about a reconciliation with the faith community, the Church, which is wounded by our sins. Religious instruction should teach this sacrament as bringing individualized direction towards spiritual growth, towards eliminating habits of sin and working for perfection.... Every Catholic, from his early years, should be instructed how to receive and best profit from the regular reception of this sacrament" (n.11).

## Materials

cloth or paper, paste, scissors...for banner making

# PRESENTATION

## Introduction

*After an opening spontaneous prayer, invite one or more children to tell the story of the prodigal son—"the young man who ran away from home."*

## Message

You are preparing to make your first confession. There are five things we do in confession, and they are like five things that the runaway young man did.

In our story, the good father stands for God. The bad son stands for everyone who commits sin.

The loving father kissing his lost son is like Jesus welcoming back a lost sinner. When we commit sin, we leave Jesus and we hurt Him. When we come back sorry, we make Him very happy. This is because He loves us.

Notice how the bad son acted. After he had sinned and was very unhappy, he **thought** of what he had done. He said to himself, "I have sinned." He was **sorry** for his sins, and he **made up his mind not to sin again.**

See, children, the first thing he did was to think back over what he had done. When we prepare for confession, we do the same thing. We find out our sins. First we ask Jesus and Mary to help us. Then we think hard what wrong we have done. We think: did I disobey God's law—at home, in church, in school, outdoors playing...?

After we have found out our sins, the next thing to do is to be sorry for them. We are sorry because we offended God and earned punishment by our sins. If we are not sorry for our sins, Jesus will not forgive them. It is easy to be sorry for our sins, if we remember that they have displeased Jesus, who loves us so much. Ask Jesus to help you to be sorry for your sins.

Suppose the bad son had come back to his father and said very saucily: "Give me some food!" Suppose he had not even said he was sorry. Do you think he would have deserved to be forgiven?... Oh no! The same is true for us. We must be sorry every time we go to confession. Without sorrow, none of our sins will be forgiven.

The third step is to make up our minds not to sin again. If we are really sorry for displeasing God, we certainly do not want to do it again!

So we think something like this: "Dear Jesus, I never want to hurt You again by being disobedient, lazy, mean, etc. I promise to keep away from all sin. I promise to stay away from the people, places and things that lead to sin." How pleased Jesus is then! That is the way to show Him how much you love Him.

Then we go into the confessional or room. And there we **tell our sins** to the priest. But we are really telling them to Jesus. And the priest says special words which mean that Jesus forgives us.

Jesus gave this great power to forgive sins to His apostles on the first Easter Sunday night. He told His special friends, the apostles: "Whose sins you shall forgive, they are forgiven" (see John 20:23). The apostles passed the same wonderful power on to the priests who took their places. That is how all priests have the power to forgive sins. When we confess our sins to them with sorrow, they forgive our sins in the name of Jesus. It is really Jesus to whom we confess our sins. And it is Jesus who forgives our sins through His priest.

We never have to worry about anything we tell a priest in confession, because he **has to** keep it a secret.

The priest tells us something to say or do to make up for our sins. This is called a **penance.** Remember the young man in the story? He said he wanted to do something to make up for hurting his father.

Why does the priest give us the penance? Well, when you do something wrong, what do you do? You try to make up for it in some way, don't you? If you make your little brother cry, you say, "I'm sorry. Don't cry. I'll play with you all afternoon." You feel a need to make up for the way you hurt him.

It's the same when we displease God by sin. We try to make up for it in some way. That is why the priest gives us a **penance,** a way to make up. The penance is not hard. Usually the priest tells us to say a few prayers. When we come out of the confessional or reconciliation room, we say them right away. Of course, good boys and girls try to make up for their sins in other ways, too. They try to be extra obedient and kind. They even try to eat things they don't like or give up a game in order to help mother more—all for the love of Jesus and to make up for their sins.

Wonderful things happen to us when we go to confession. We grow closer to God and to all His people. We share more fully in God's own life. We receive more help from God to be better.

Sometimes people commit mortal sins and lose God's life completely. When they make a good confession, God gives back this life again. How wonderful confession is!

## In the Textbook

*Carefully read the lesson, explaining the difficult words, such as:*

sacrament—a special meeting with Jesus, who gives us grace even though we don't see Him

confession—telling our sins to the priest, so he can forgive us in the name of Jesus

Penance—the sacrament of God's loving forgiveness

penance—prayers we say or something else that we

do to make up a little for our sins
absolve — to set free from sin
absolution — the freeing of a person from sin
words of absolution — the words by which a priest,
    in Jesus' name, frees a person from sin

*Answer any questions that the children may ask about confession, even if the material more properly belongs to the next lesson.*

## REINFORCEMENT

### Summary

Jesus gave priests the power to forgive sins in His name. When we go to confession our sins are forgiven by Jesus and we grow in grace. Penance is the sacrament of peace and joy.

### Application

I will learn the five things I need to do to receive the sacrament of Penance. I will go to confession well.

### Activity

*Using "make-a-banner kits," scraps of material, or even wallpaper samples, each child can make a banner with his "motto for first Penance." Some ideas:*
I will go back to my Father (Lk. 15:18).
God is love (1 Jn. 4:8).
God loves me.
Father, forgive me.
Jesus is the Good Shepherd.
The Lord is my Shepherd (Ps. 23:1).
Peace — Joy!

### Assignment

*Part of the assignment refers to the five things we need to do to receive the sacrament of Penance. Note* that knowing our sins always comes first; saying or doing our penance always comes last. Because sorrow and resolution always go together and should accompany confession, there is no strict chronological order for the three middle steps.

Hence, the children do not need to memorize these three steps in any particular order.

## ADDITIONAL AIDS AND ACTIVITIES

### As a Class or Family

**Penitential Celebration.** If possible, arrange all the chairs around a low table bearing one or more candelabra or some single candles.
All stand.
Opening song. This and the closing song may be any that the children choose. (Have your cassettes and records ready . . . . )
All sit. The teacher or a helper lights the candles.
Teacher:
When we were baptized, each of us received a lighted candle. Light makes the world more beautiful. We ourselves are like light. When we live as God's good children, we shine in the world and make it more beautiful. But when we fail to love God and others, our light becomes less bright.
All stand.
Teacher:
Let us listen to a reading from the holy Gospel (Matthew 5:13 and 16).
Jesus said: "You are the light of the world . . . . Your light must shine before men so that they may see goodness in your acts and give praise to your heavenly Father."
This is the Gospel of the Lord.
All: Praise to you, Lord Jesus Christ.
All sit.
Teacher:
Now let us think quietly about the way our light is burning . . . .

*(Pause between the questions.)*
Have I done something that I wish I had not done?
Do I do that wrong thing often?
When I was saying my prayers, did I think of other
things on purpose?
Have I missed Sunday Mass?
Have I gone to Mass late on purpose?
Have I talked and fooled around at Mass?
Have I failed to obey my parents and teachers?
Have I spoken to them unkindly?
How have I treated other people, including other boys
and girls....
Have I been mean?
When others have been mean to me, have I tried
to "get even"?
Have I failed to share my things when I should have
shared them?
Have I called names or said other unkind words?
Have I taken or broken something that was not mine?
Have I watched bad programs or said bad words?
Have I told lies?
*Helper (or teacher):*
Let us think about what these wrong things do to
us. Every time we do something wrong or fail to do some-
thing we know we should do, our light becomes less
bright.
*As you talk, put out most of the candles.* Every...
fault...makes...our...light...less...bright. Do you see
what our faults do to us?
*Teacher or helper:*
Let us stand and tell God that we are sorry for what
has happened to our light. Together let us say the Act
of Contrition.
*All stand and recite the version that the children have
learned. The teacher or helper re-lights the candles.*
*Teacher:*
See—the light is bright again. Jesus gave us the
sacrament of Penance so that our light would always be
bright. Let us sing a happy song to thank Him for being
so good to us.
*Closing hymn—chosen by the children.*

## *At Home or in the Classroom*

**Story.** Once a man went to confession to the great St. Anthony of Padua. This man had committed many, many big sins, but now he was very, very sorry for them. In fact he felt so bad about having offended Jesus that he could not even talk! Even though he was a grown-up man he cried and cried.

St. Anthony said to him, "You may write your sins down on a piece of paper, if you want."

The man agreed and he wrote all his sins on a sheet of paper. Then he handed it to St. Anthony. The saint began to read it — and guess what happened!

That man noticed that as the saint read, the lines disappeared. Each sin disappeared from the paper as the saint read it. When he finished reading, the paper was all white again! There was not one sin left on it! Imagine! God made this special miracle just to show us how our souls look to Him after we make a good confession. No sins are left. Jesus takes them all away.

# 12
# How To Receive
# the Sacrament
# of Penance

## TO PARENTS AND TEACHERS

The time for the child's first reception of the sacrament of Penance has arrived. Concentration on the procedure to be followed should not overshadow the importance of the proper dispositions — love, sorrow, resolution to do better. The child should be made keenly aware that in this sacrament he will meet Jesus, who will lovingly forgive him, give him a greater share in God's own life, and strengthen him to avoid sin. If parent and teacher keep these facts in mind, they will transmit the proper attitudes to the children under their care.

## TO PARENTS ESPECIALLY

The child should be encouraged to express his failings in his own words. If you think he could use your help in discovering his faults, the areas of obedience, honesty and truthfulness might especially be considered.

# PREPARATION

## Theme and Aim

There is a certain way to receive the sacrament of Penance.

I will learn what to do and say.

## Key Words

> commit
> displease
> act of contrition
> endures

## Suggested Preparatory Reading

**FROM THE GENERAL CATECHETICAL DIRECTORY:**

"Catechesis will have the duty of presenting the seven sacraments according to their full meaning.

"First, they must be presented as sacraments of faith. Of themselves they certainly express the efficacious will of Christ the Savior; but men, on their part, must show a sincere will to respond to God's love and mercy. Hence, catechesis must concern itself with the acquisition of proper dispositions, with the stimulation of sincerity and  generosity for a worthy reception of the sacraments.

"Second, the sacraments must be presented, each according to its own nature and end, not only as remedies for sin and its consequences, but especially as sources of grace in individuals and in communities, so that the entire dispensation of grace in the life of the faithful may be related in some way to the sacramental economy" (n. 56).

The official Rite of Penance (if this is not available at your local book store or a library, write to: USCC Publications Office, 1312 Mass. Ave., N.W., Washington, D.C. 20005).

## Materials

> Rite of Penance leaflets
> optional—improvised "confessional" and/or "reconciliation room"

## PRESENTATION

### Introduction

Pray the Our Father or sing one of the songs the children have learned, such as "God's Rules for Me" or "In the Eyes of God."

Discuss the meaning of the important words in the last chapter: sacrament, confession, Penance and penance, absolve, absolution.

### Message

Today's lesson is about how to go to confession. If possible, the instruction could take place where the actual confessions will be held. If this cannot be done, try to simulate — in home or classroom — the set-up of the confessional and/or reconciliation room used in your parish.

Have the children open their textbooks to lesson 12 and read with you. As you read, show them where they will kneel, sit, etc.; when they will make the sign of the cross...in other words, act out the part of the person going to confession. Do this once all the way through for confession through a screen. Repeat the procedure for confession face-to-face. Make sure, however, that the children understand they are to make their first confession either one way or the other — not both!

## REINFORCEMENT

### Summary

To receive the sacrament of Penance well, we think about what we have done wrong, tell our sins to the priest and say an act of contrition. We are sorry for our sins and intend not to do them again. We do or say our penance.

### Application

I will learn how to go to confession. I will be sure that I know a prayer of sorrow.

## Activity

*Have the children practice for confession, using their religion books or Penance leaflets and going through everything (except for the accusation of sins) one by one in the same setting(s) which you used in showing them how to go to confession.*

## Assignment

*Remind the children that they will say an act of contrition when going to confession. Explain that they may use one of the acts of contrition from the Rite of Penance (see official Rite, or the Rite of Penance leaflet, or his activity book); or he may make one up; or he may use the act of contrition that the whole class was to have learned recently.*

## Further Points About Telling Our Sins

If you say your sins in the confessional, talk softly so that only the priest will hear you. Start with the bigger sins first. If a person has mortal sins, he should start with them, and he must say all the mortal sins he can remember that he has not confessed before. He must say how many times he has committed each sin. It is a big sin to leave out a mortal sin **on purpose.** If a person does that, he has made a *bad* confession. *Explain that it is not necessary to confess all our venial sins, but it is better.* If we **forget** a mortal sin, all our sins are forgiven anyway, because we did not do it on purpose. The next time we go to confession, we say: "Father, I forgot this sin (and we say it) in my last confession."

Of course, people do not commit mortal sins casually, so when we go to confession we will be telling venial sins most of the time, even, we hope, all the time.

If a person feels ashamed to confess his sins, what should he do? He should think of how much Jesus loves him.

If you do not know how to say a certain sin, ask the priest to help you. Say, "Father, I have a sin that I don't know how to say." He will help you by asking questions.

If you are not sure whether something was a sin, ask Father in confession.

# Communitarian
# Celebration of Penance

## Introductory Note:

Communitarian celebrations of Penance serve to awaken the children to the social dimensions of sin and reconciliation. Each of our sins is both a refusal to love God and a refusal to love His people. Communitarian celebrations develop awareness of the Christian life as a life of love.

The children and their parents should be familiarized beforehand with the hymns to be sung, the general procedure to be followed and the form of the Act of Contrition which all will recite. It would be well for at least some of the parents and other persons accompanying the children to also go to confession during the celebration. Perhaps, too, a member of each family could bring the youngster's baptismal candle or another blessed candle, so that it may be lighted at the conclusion of the celebration, to emphasize the relationship of this sacrament with that of Baptism.

Provision will have to be made for those children who might not be able to bring anyone with them. The classroom teacher and various helpers could obtain and carry candles for them, exchange the sign of peace with them, etc.

## The Celebration:

Place: the parish church — festively decorated with some of the children's own handiwork. A large crucifix should be visible in the sanctuary — if possible, in a position

*where all can approach it and kiss it at the conclusion
of the celebration. When everyone has arrived, the chil-
dren enter the church, accompanied by their parents and
other members of the parish community, such as god-
parents, relatives and family friends.*
*All stand.*
*Opening hymn: an entrance hymn, such as the first and
second verses of "Be Glad" on the beatitudes, or "Law of
Love" from the cassette "Sing! Sing! Sing!" by the
Daughters of St. Paul.*
*All sit.*
*Priest:*

   We priests want to welcome you boys and girls who
are going to receive the sacrament of Penance for the
first time. We also welcome your parents, your godparents
and your other relatives and friends. This is a very·happy
day. It is a day on which you will grow closer to Jesus and
to all God's people.
*All stand.*

*Priest or Parent:*

   Let us listen to a reading from the holy Gospel.
   *He reads from Luke 15:11-24—the prodigal son.*
   This is the Gospel of the Lord.
*All:* Praise to You, Lord Jesus Christ.
*All sit.*
*Priest:*

   When the prodigal son returned home to his father,
there was a great celebration. We, too, are celebrating
today, because it is the day of your first confession. Baptism has already brought us the love of Jesus and the love
of God's family. Today, and every time we go to confession, Jesus comes to forgive us and to love us more deeply.
And we grow closer to all God's family.

   Let us remember in the silence of our hearts the faults
that we think have displeased God our loving Father the
most. These are the faults that we will tell in confession.
*Silent reflection.*

*Priest:*

   Now we will say an Act of Contrition together—all
of us. As we say it, we will think of how sorry we are for

having displeased God, our loving Father. And we will promise Him that we will try to be better from now on.
*Act of Contrition.*

*Following the Act of Contrition, the priest might invite the children to exchange a sign of peace and love with their parents, godparents, etc., as a way of showing their desire for the forgiveness of God and all His people.*
*Priest:*

Now you and some of your parents and friends will go to confession. While waiting before or after confession, we will praise our loving Father by singing hymns.

*As many priests as possible should be available for the children's confessions, and the children should be free to choose the confessor to whom they will go. Appropriate hymns, such as "Because You Loved Me" from the record/cassette "Where Your Treasure Is" and a version of the Good Shepherd Psalm, 23 (22), may be sung at intervals until all the children and some of the adults have gone to confession.*

*Priest:*

Now in silence we will thank Jesus for His great love in coming to us in the sacrament of Penance. If you have not yet said your penance, this would be a good time to do so.

*After a suitable pause, the celebration may be concluded by filing up to kiss the crucifix and — if it seems appropriate for the liturgical season — by lighting the children's candles from the paschal candle. (The candles are extinguished after the closing hymn. They might be lighted again at the next family meal as a reminder of the joy of this day.)*

*Concluding hymn: "Sing to the Lord" from the cassette "Sing! Sing! Sing!"*

*(A party for the children and those accompanying them would be another means of emphasizing the joy of this occasion.)*

# 13
# Jesus Chose To Stay With Us Always

## TO PARENTS AND TEACHERS—CATECHESIS REGARDING THE HOLY EUCHARIST

"The most Blessed Eucharist contains the entire spiritual wealth of the Church—that is, Christ Himself, our Passover and living Bread. By the action of the Holy Spirit, through His very flesh living and life-giving, He offers life to men—who are thus invited and encouraged to offer themselves, their labors and all created things together with Him.... The faithful, already marked with the seal of Baptism and Confirmation, are through the reception of the Eucharist fully joined to the Body of Christ" (Vatican II—Decree on the Ministry and Life of Priests, n. 5).

In lessons 13-22, treating of "the summit toward which the activity of the Church is directed...the font from which all her power flows" (Vatican II), the children are taught about the origin of the Eucharistic Celebration making present the paschal mystery of Christ. They learn what it means to share fully in the Eucharist.

Among the points to keep in mind when teaching these lessons are:

—First Communion is not only a goal; it is also a beginning. Like first confession, it should initiate a new period of spiritual growth.

—First Communion is not the child's first contact with Christ. By means of the grace of Baptism and Penance and as a result of the child's developing prayer life, Jesus is already living and active within him.

— On the day of first Communion the child is admitted into full participation in the Eucharistic Celebration. He should take part in Sunday Mass regularly from that time on, as he should from the age of seven when he reaches the use of reason.

—The reception of Holy Communion is not to be viewed as an isolated event. It should always be seen within the context of the Mass.

—In the Mass, we listen to God's Word. Jesus gives Himself to the Father and then He gives Himself to us. We give ourselves with Jesus and receive Him from the Father.

—Communion brings us closer to Jesus and to all God's people. It is a promise of the love and joy that we will share in heaven.

## REGARDING CHAPTER 13 IN PARTICULAR—

The simple faith of children does not doubt, so it needs no proofs. Let us take care, therefore, to present this great sacrament with a lively faith. The Holy Eucharist is Jesus, *really* in our midst; He is the great Friend of children.

## PREPARATION

### Theme and Aim

Jesus promised that He would be our bread of life. At the Last Supper He changed bread and wine into His body and blood—the Holy Eucharist.

"I will thank Jesus for the Holy Eucharist."

### Key Words

| | |
|---|---|
| Last Supper | Holy Eucharist |
| apostles | Holy Communion |

## Suggested Preparatory Reading

**FROM THE GENERAL CATECHETICAL DIRECTORY:**

"In catechesis on the sacraments, much importance should be placed on the explanation of the signs. Catechesis should lead the faithful through the visible signs to ponder God's invisible mysteries of salvation" (n. 57).

**SCRIPTURE PASSAGES FOR REFLECTION:**

*The Eucharist was prefigured in the manna (Exodus 16:15 and following)*

*—was prefigured in the parable of the wedding feast (Matthew 22:1 and following)*

*—was instituted by Jesus at the Last Supper (Luke 22:14, 20)*

*—Jesus is the living and life-giving Bread (John 6:51-58).*

# PRESENTATION

## Introduction

*Spontaneous prayer.*
*Before moving on to the second sacrament that the children are to receive this year, you might wish to make sure that they have no further questions about the sacrament of Penance. Encourage them to receive it frequently—once a month or even more often.*
*Ask what other sacrament they are going to receive this year and what they understand by "Communion." Clarify any hazy notions. Also explain that they will be able to receive Communion often and that every Communion—not just the first one—is important, because in Communion we receive Jesus.*

## Message

This story tells us how Communion began.

Once, Jesus and His apostles got into a fishing boat that one of the apostles owned. They sailed across a big lake called the Sea of Galilee. They wanted to be away from the crowds and talk with one another. Usually so many people were following Jesus that the apostles could hardly even get near Him!

When Jesus and His friends came to another section of the lakeshore, they left the boat and started to climb up a mountainside. And then, can you guess what happened? They saw people coming along the shore of the lake. These people were looking for Jesus. They had seen Him get into the boat and had walked along the shore looking for Him.

Jesus looked at the people. There were hundreds of them, and He knew how much they needed Him. Some of them were sick. So He began to work miracles to make the sick people well. All of them needed to know more about our Father in heaven and what we must do to reach lasting happiness with God. So Jesus started to teach them. He taught and taught, until it was almost sunset.

The apostles started to get worried. They were out in the country, and the people certainly were hungry. Would they have to go to bed hungry out there in the fields?

The apostles talked to one another about it. Then some of them came up to Jesus.

"Master," they said, "maybe You should send these people away so that they can go to the farms and villages nearby and buy themselves something to eat."

Jesus smiled. "There isn't any need to send them away," He said. "Give them some food yourselves." Then He spoke to the apostle who was called Philip. "Where shall we buy bread for these people to eat?" Jesus asked.

Philip answered, "It would take a lot of money even to buy enough bread to give everyone a little piece each."

"How many loaves do you have?" Jesus asked.

Another apostle, named Andrew, answered, "There's a boy here who has five loaves of bread and two dried fish. But what good is that? There are too many people!"

"Bring the bread and fish here," said Jesus. Then He added, "Have the people sit down in groups—about 50 people in each group."

Jesus picked up the five loaves of bread and the two fish. He said a prayer. After that, He broke the loaves and started to pass them around to the apostles. And the apostles took them and gave them to the groups of people.

Can you imagine...? The apostles never ran out of bread to give to the people until everyone had enough to eat! And it was the same way with the fish!

All of the people ate until they had had enough. It was a miracle!

When the meal was over, Jesus said, "Go and collect the bread that is left, so that nothing will go to waste." The apostles went and collected the bread and brought it back to Jesus in baskets. They were big baskets, and there were twelve of them—all full. The apostles collected some fish too. So they ended up with more than they had started with.

Can you imagine how surprised everyone was?

The next day Jesus talked about the great wonder He had worked with the bread. He had given the people ordinary bread. But Jesus promised to give a greater bread. He promised to give Himself. He said:

"I myself am the living bread come down from heaven.
If anyone eats this bread
he shall live forever;
the bread I will give
is my flesh, for the life of the world."

Jesus kept His promise, as He always does. The night before He died, He ate a special meal with His friends, the apostles. We call that meal the Last Supper.

Jesus knew He was going to die the next day. But He wanted to stay with His apostles and all of us in a special way. So He took bread and blessed it. Then He said, "This is my body. Take and eat."

Jesus had changed the bread into His own body, so He could be close to the apostles and give them strength! Jesus was able to do this because He is God.

Then Jesus blessed a cup of wine. He said, "Take and drink. This is my blood."

Jesus had changed bread and wine into His own body and blood. The apostles received the body and blood of Jesus, which still looked like bread and wine. This was their first Holy Communion.

Jesus also said something else to His apostles. He said, "Do this as a remembrance of me." With these words He gave priests the power to do just what He had done: at every Mass, priests say special words, and Jesus changes bread and wine into His own body and blood!

And at every Mass Jesus comes to each person who receives Holy Communion. He makes God's own life grow in each person. Do you know the reason why Jesus is able to do this? *Pupil response.* Yes, Jesus is God. And because He is God, He can do all things.

We call the body and blood of Jesus by a special name—**the Holy Eucharist.**

How much Jesus loves us! In the Holy Eucharist He gives us His own body and blood as food for our souls. You know that if you want to grow big and strong, you have to eat, don't you? Your body needs food or it cannot live. Well, you have to grow strong in being good, too, and strong in avoiding sin. You need heavenly bread. Jesus is our heavenly food. During the sacrifice of the Mass, He makes bread and wine become His body and blood. Then we can go to receive Him in Holy Communion. When we receive Holy Communion, we have Jesus right inside us.

This is wonderful, isn't it? Jesus could do this because He is God, and God can do all things. No ordinary person could do something so wonderful. Only God could do it. And Jesus did it because He loves us.

## *In the Textbook*

*Read lesson 13.*

## REINFORCEMENT

### *Summary*

Jesus is the Bread of Life. He is present in the Holy Eucharist.

## Application

"I will thank Jesus for the Holy Eucharist."

## Assignment

*The activity book work will require careful explanation.*

# ADDITIONAL AIDS AND ACTIVITIES

## In the Classroom

### Paraliturgical Celebration.

*All stand.*

*Opening song: "Jesus, We Believe"*

*All sit.*
*Teacher:*

Today we will read from God's Book about a wonderful event that happened before the Last Supper and a promise that Jesus made. We will read from the holy Gospel. Usually we stand while the Gospel is read, but today you may sit, so that it will be easier for you to listen with attention.

The Lord be with you.

*Class:*

And also with you.

*Teacher:*

A reading from the holy Gospel according to John.

*Class:*

Glory to you, Lord.

*Teacher:* (John 6:1-13)

Soon after this, the people asked Jesus for more bread and He said: (John 6:51; 54-56)

This is the Gospel of the Lord.

*Class:*

Praise to you, Lord Jesus Christ.

*Teacher:*

Let us talk about this section of the Gospel.

What happened after Jesus multiplied the loaves of bread and they collected all the scraps? (The people asked Jesus for more bread.)

What did Jesus tell the people? (That He Himself is the living bread — the bread of life.)

When was the first time that Jesus ever gave Himself to anyone as Communion? (At the Last Supper.)

*You might wish to ask other questions, reviewing points that the children especially seem to need help with.*

*The following Gospel-prayer will be found in the activity book on the second page of poems and prayers:*

*Teacher:*

Now we will pray, asking Jesus to come to us often in Holy Communion. You say: Lord, give us this bread always.

*Class:*

Lord, give us this bread always.

*First Leader:*

Jesus said: "I am the bread of life."

*Class:*

Lord, give us this bread always.

*Second Leader:*

"He who comes to me shall not hunger."

*Class:*

Lord, give us this bread always.

*Third Leader:*

"He who believes in me shall not thirst."

*Class:*
Lord, give us this bread always.
*Fourth Leader:*
"He who eats this bread shall live forever."
*Class:*
Lord, give us this bread always.
*Fifth Leader:*
"He who eats my flesh and drinks my blood stays in me, and I in him."
*Class:*
Lord, give us this bread always.
*Teacher:*
Let us end our celebration by singing a song about the Holy Eucharist. *Closing hymn: "God Within Us" from the cassette "Children, Sing!"*

## In the Classroom

Invite the children to practice the little play "The Bread of Life," which they will find in the poem and song section of their activity books.

Perhaps they could put this play on for their relatives or for another class. Each costume: a simple tunic plus a headpiece made of a square of cloth held on by a head-band.

# 14
# Every Sunday We Celebrate Jesus' Resurrection

## TO PARENTS AND TEACHERS

Impress on the children the fact that Sunday is the day God established for the good of our soul. It is the Lord's day, the day of special union with Him.

And weekly Mass is a must.

## TO PARENTS ESPECIALLY

Make sure that Sunday is free of work or business that would inhibit the worship to be given to God, the joy proper to the Lord's Day, or the due relaxation of mind and body.

## PREPARATION

### Theme and Aim

Jesus rose from the dead! Every Sunday we celebrate Jesus' resurrection at Mass.

"I will remember that Sundays are special."

### Key Words

resurrection
Mass

## Suggested Preparatory Reading

**FROM THE CONSTITUTION ON THE SACRED LITURGY:**

"By a tradition handed down from the apostles which takes its origin from the very day of Christ's resurrection, the Church celebrates the paschal mystery every eighth day. With good reason this, then, bears the name of the Lord's day, or Sunday. For on this day Christ's faithful should come together in one place so that, by hearing the word of God and taking part in the Eucharist, they may call to mind the passion, the resurrection, and the glorification of the Lord Jesus, and may thank God who 'has begotten them again, through the resurrection of Jesus Christ from the dead, unto a living hope' (1 Pt. 1:3). Hence the Lord's day is the original feast day, and it should be proposed to the piety of the faithful and taught to them so that it may become in fact a day of joy and of freedom from work" (n. 106).

**SCRIPTURE READINGS FOR REFLECTION:**

— *Jesus appears to Mary Magdalene and entrusts her with the mission of announcing His resurrection to the disciples (John 20:11-18).*
— *Jesus rose "early on the first day of the week" (Mt. 28:1; Mk. 16:9; Lk. 24:1; Jn. 20:1), actually Sunday.*
— *The Sunday celebration of the risen Christ can be traced back to the beginnings of Christianity (Jn. 20:26-27; Acts 20:6-12).*

# PRESENTATION

## Introduction

*Invite the children to tell about the multiplication of the loaves, Jesus' promise, and the Last Supper. Make sure that they realize that the Eucharist is Jesus.*

We have the Eucharist because of the Last Supper and Jesus' death on the cross. We celebrate the Eucharist (Mass) on **Sunday** because of Jesus' resurrection.

## Message

On the first Sunday after Jesus died, in the very early morning, the apostles and Jesus' other followers were sad, because they had not really understood His promise that He would come back to life again.

That morning some good women who had followed Jesus from one town to another when He was teaching went to visit the tomb where Jesus had been buried. On the way, they heard a big noise. It was like an earthquake. And when they got to the tomb, what do you think they saw? The tomb was open and it was empty! Then they saw an angel. The angel said, "Jesus is risen! He is not here!"

How happy those good friends of Jesus were when they heard that! Jesus had really risen from the dead!

What does that mean — to rise from the dead? It means that Jesus came back to life again. When a person dies, the body cannot move any more. The eyes cannot see, the tongue cannot speak — the body has no life. The soul that was inside the body goes on living, but the body is dead. When a person dies, he cannot come to life again. His body is put in a grave. The body of Jesus was put in a grave, too. But **He did come to life again,** because He is God, and God can do anything. This great miracle is called the resurrection of Jesus.

One of Jesus' friends was Mary Magdalene.

On Easter Sunday, before she knew that Jesus had risen from the dead, Mary was crying near Jesus' tomb. She thought that someone had come and taken Jesus' body away. How sad she was!

Suddenly, she saw a man standing in front of her. It was Jesus, but Mary did not know it. She thought He was the gardener of the place. "Sir," she said, "if you have taken Jesus away, tell me where you have laid Him, and I will take Him away." Poor Mary! She did not know that Jesus was alive — and that He was right in front of her! Then Jesus called her by name: "Mary!" Oh, what joy went through her heart at the sound of that dear voice! She knew now that it was Jesus! He was alive again! How happy Mary was!

How happy **all** of Jesus' followers were when they saw Him!

Every Sunday we celebrate Jesus' resurrection. We do this at Mass.

The Mass is a wonderful prayer in which we join with Jesus in praying to our heavenly Father.

At every Mass, we have a holy meal like the Last Supper.

At every Mass, Jesus offers Himself to His Father for us, the way He did when He died on the cross. He frees us from slavery to sin and makes us His people in a special way.

At every Mass, God's family remembers that Jesus died for us and came back to life again for us.

Adults and children who are seven or have made their first Communion should go to Mass every Sunday.

It would be a mortal sin to miss Mass on Sunday through our own fault.

We must be present at the whole Mass, from the beginning to the end.

It would be a venial sin if through our own fault we were to come a little late for Mass — if, for example, we came during the readings or homily.

Of course, it would not be a sin at all if it were very hard for a person to go to Mass, either because he was very far from the church, or because he was ill, or because he had to take care of someone who was sick, or some similar good excuse.

Let us always remember that each of us has a place in our parish church. By that I mean that we are members of God's family, and our heavenly Father wants to see each of us near His altar every Sunday to take part in offering the Mass. We should never think that because ours is a large parish family, God will "never miss me." How mistaken we would be! God loves each of us and wants each of us to show Him love and honor on His day. He has many blessings to give each of us at Mass, too. We would displease our heavenly Father greatly if we ever skipped

Mass or came in very late through our own fault. And who would want to do that? Our heavenly Father has given us so much, and our Lord Jesus offers Himself for us at every Mass! The least we can do is to show our thankfulness by lovingly worshiping Him on His day or on Saturday evening, which counts as Sunday.

Once we have come home from Sunday Mass, how do we keep the Lord's day holy? Our heavenly Father asks us not to work, as on the other six days of the week. Instead, Sunday is to be a day of extra prayer, rest for your parents, and happy times for the whole family. It is a joyful day.

## In the Textbook

*Read lesson 14.*

## REINFORCEMENT

### Summary

Sunday is a day of joy, on which we celebrate Jesus' resurrection. We celebrate it at Mass, where Jesus talks to us, offers His sacrifice for us, and comes to us in Holy Communion.

### Application

"I will remember that Sundays are special"; I will pray well at Mass.

### Activity

*Teach the children some hymns that may be sung during the Eucharistic Celebration.*

## Assignment

*The children might start their homework in class so that you may help anyone who finds difficulty.*

## Prayer

*Leader:* This is the day that the Lord has made.
*Class:* Let us be glad and rejoice.
*Leader:* Give praise to the Lord for He is good.
*Class:* Let us be glad and rejoice.
*Leader:* Christ is risen. Alleluia! Alleluia!
*Class:* Let us be glad and rejoice.

# ADDITIONAL AIDS AND ACTIVITIES

## At Home or in the Classroom

**Story.** There was once a poor old man who lived far from the church in his town. He used to walk to Mass every Sunday and even every day of the week. The older he grew, the harder it became for him to walk so far to Mass. So he decided to sell his house and buy a house nearer the church. The Sunday morning before he was to move to his new home, he was walking to church as usual. Suddenly he heard, "One, two, three, four...!" The old man stopped, not knowing what to think. He turned to look behind. No one was in sight. So he began to walk again.

"Five, six, seven, eight...." Who could it be? The old man looked all around, but no one could he see. So again he began to walk on.

"Nine, ten, eleven...." This time, the old man called out loudly, "Who is it? Who are you, I say!"

"I am your guardian angel," came the answer. "I am counting the steps you are taking to go to holy Mass!"

Then it was that the old man understood how very pleased God was with the sacrifice he was making to walk so far to Mass. So he decided not to move nearer the church, after all.

## In the Classroom

**Dramatization.** Mary Magdalene and two other women approach the tomb. When they find it empty, Mary Magdalene runs away crying. The other women listen with joy to the words of the angel. Then they start to go to tell the apostles. Jesus meets them and they bow in homage. After Jesus exits, the women also exit. Peter and John come running in, followed by Mary Magdalene. Peter and John find the tomb empty. They look puzzled and walk off stage slowly. Mary Magdalene remains weeping at the tomb. The angels talk to her. Then Jesus comes up behind her. After the dialogue between them, Jesus exits, followed by Mary.

# 15
# What Happens at Mass

## TO PARENTS AND TEACHERS — CATECHESIS ON THE EUCHARISTIC CELEBRATION

Man owes God adoration, thanksgiving and love. These religious acts taken together are called **worship.** Worship is internal (for example, when one thinks of God) and external (for example, when one kneels); public, that which the Church offers God through ministers (for example, the Eucharistic Celebration), and private (for example, the rosary).

The whole man—body and soul—depends upon God. Therefore, the honor which we owe to God should not be limited to inner feelings. It must also show itself outwardly, so that the body, as well as the spirit, will pay homage to the Creator. Furthermore, man lives in society; hence, his duty of giving God **public worship.**

The central act of all Christian worship is the Eucharistic Celebration. It is the worship of the Father, accomplished once and for all by Christ the Priest, but still continued by Him in the priestly community that is the Church.

"The Church earnestly desires that Christ's faithful, when present at this mystery of faith, should not be there as strangers or silent spectators; on the contrary, through a good understanding of the rites and prayers they should take part in the sacred action conscious of what they are doing, with devotion and full collaboration. They should be instructed by God's word and be nourished at the table of the Lord's body; they should give thanks to God; by offering the Immaculate Victim, not only through the hands of the priest, but also with him, they should learn also to offer themselves; through Christ the Mediator, they should be drawn day by day into ever more perfect union with God and with each other, so that finally God may be all in all.''

*Constitution on the Sacred Liturgy, n. 48*

Initiation of children to the Mass may be accomplished in four ways:

— attendance at the Eucharistic Celebration;
— participation in paraliturgies;
— systematic instruction;
— active participation in the Eucharistic Celebration.

A combination of all four brings fruitful results.

Usually when children prepare for first Communion they are already accustomed to going to Mass. Their presence at Mass, however, is generally passive. It is the task of the religion teacher and of the parent to lead them from mere presence to active participation in the Eucharistic Liturgy.

## TO PARENTS ESPECIALLY

If your child is not yet accustomed to attending Mass, begin to take him now.

Help him learn to follow it with his Mass book or missalette.

## PREPARATION

### Theme and Aim

Many different things take place during the Mass. "I will learn about the Mass."

## Key Words

| | |
|---|---|
| rite | faith |
| liturgy | creed |
| Word | faithful |
| homily | Consecration |
| profession | |

## Suggested Preparatory Reading

**FROM THE CONSTITUTION ON THE SACRED LITURGY:**

"At the Last Supper, on the night when He was betrayed, our Savior instituted the Eucharistic Sacrifice of His body and blood. He did this in order to perpetuate the sacrifice of the cross throughout the centuries until He should come again, and so to entrust to His beloved spouse, the Church, a memorial of His death and resurrection: a sacrament of love, a sign of unity, a bond of charity, a paschal banquet in which Christ is eaten, the mind is filled with grace, and a pledge of future glory is given to us" (n. 47).

## Materials

homemade posters summing up the parts of the Mass (see "message")
optional —
a few building blocks and chessmen
homemade posters of vestments
and sacred vessels

# PRESENTATION

## Introduction

*Our Father.*
*Review the material covered in the last lesson, basing your questions on the activity book homework.*

## Message

*Since today's lesson consists in a general view of the Mass, it would be well to break the material up by means of homemade posters and treat it very simply.*

*The four posters would read as follows:*

ENTRANCE RITE
>   Greeting
>   Prayer for forgiveness
>   One or two other prayers

LITURGY OF THE WORD
>   Readings
>   Homily
>   Profession of Faith
>   Prayer of the Faithful

LITURGY OF THE EUCHARIST
>   Preparation of the Gifts
>   Eucharistic Prayer
>   Communion

DISMISSAL
>   Blessing

## First Option— Presentation of the Lesson in Church

*This would be ideal, especially if a priest, deacon, lector or teenage altar boy could be present to explain— and, to some extent, act out—the sequence of the Mass while you hold up the posters one by one and point to the words.*

*Before, during or after this enactment of the order of Mass, the children could also be brought into the sanctuary and sacristy and familiarized with the appearance and purpose (not necessarily the names) of the sacred vessels and some of the vestments. (See the activity for this lesson.)*

## Second Option—
## Presentation of the Lesson in the Classroom

*If circumstances do not permit option one, follow the same procedure in the classroom. Your desk could serve as the altar. Or instead of taking the part of the priest yourself, you could work with building blocks—one for the altar, one for (each) lectern—and a few small figures, such as a bishop and some pawns from a chess set. The children's text can be your guide; it will be enough to give a general idea of what the priest and people do during each part of the Mass. (If you wish to go into more detail, see "A More Detailed Description of the Mass" below.)*
*Again use the posters, as suggested for option one.*

## Words To Explain

rite—a ceremony for worshiping God

liturgy—special worship given to God by a group of people

Word—the Bible, the Holy Book in which God speaks to us

homily—an important talk that the priest gives during the Mass

profession—declaration

faith—belief

creed—a prayer of belief

faithful—the members of God's Family, the Church (especially those who are not priests)

Consecration—the part of the Mass in which bread and wine become the body and blood of Jesus

## Optional—
## A More Detailed Description of the Mass

In the first part of holy Mass God teaches us with His holy words. When Mass begins, the priest makes the sign of the cross and we make it, too. Then he says prayers to prepare to offer Mass well. Sometimes we sing a hymn to God at the beginning of Mass, and then with the priest we ask God to forgive our sins. Next, all together we say out loud the beautiful prayer called the "Glory to God" to praise and thank the Blessed Trinity. After this, the priest reads two lessons from God's Holy Bible. God teaches us through these readings from His holy word. It is as though we were in the schoolroom where Jesus is the teacher. We pay attention while the priest reads and we ask Jesus to help us understand.

Sometimes, the priest will explain the word of God to us. We sit down to listen carefully. Jesus speaks to us through His priest. Afterwards, we stand to say the **Creed.** God has spoken to us and we say that we believe all He has taught us.

The Liturgy of the Eucharist is the second part of the Mass.

At the part of the Mass that is called the Preparation of the Gifts, bread, water and wine are brought to the altar. If the basket is passed, we put in an offering of some money to help God's priests do good.

The next prayer we say all together is a prayer of praise. We say it standing: "Holy! holy! holy!" Then we kneel down because Jesus is about to become present on the altar. He is about to offer Himself as a sacrifice to His Father for us as He did on the cross.

The most important part of the Mass is the **Consecration.** This is the time when the priest says the words that change the bread and wine into the body and blood of Jesus.

The priest says the words of Jesus: "This is my body." And the bread becomes the body of Jesus. We offer Jesus and ourselves to God our Father.

Then the priest says the words of Jesus: "This is the cup of my blood." And the wine becomes the blood of Jesus. We adore Jesus here on the altar.

A little while afterwards, the priest raises up both the chalice and the holy Host. He offers a prayer of honor and glory to God our Father through His Son, Jesus Christ. At the end of the prayer we say, "Amen," to show that we, too, are offering praise and glory to God, through Jesus.

Now comes the time when God our Father offers us His great gift—Jesus in Holy Communion. First we stand

and say the "Our Father" all together. We are God's family and God our Father is pleased to see us praying together. Before we receive Jesus, we give the Sign of Peace. Then we say another prayer out loud. We ask Jesus to forgive us our sins. We say, "Lamb of God, you take away the sins of the world, have mercy on us!" Once people used to offer animals, such as lambs, as a sacrifice to God. We call Jesus the lamb of God, because He offered Himself to God as a sacrifice.

At the **Communion** of the Mass, the priest receives Jesus in the sacrament of the Holy Eucharist. We may receive Jesus, too. The Holy Eucharist is a great sacrament. In it we receive Jesus.

Just before we receive Holy Communion, the priest holds up the holy Host. He says: "This is the Lamb of God who takes away the sins of the world. Happy are those who are called to his supper." All together we say a prayer that means: Jesus, before You come to me, make my soul beautiful to receive You.

We have offered Jesus to God the Father. Now God the Father gives Him back to us in Holy Communion. Jesus fills us with His grace and many blessings.

We may sing a hymn at Communion time. We ask Jesus to make us love Him and others more and more. All the people who receive Jesus in Holy Communion are very close to each other. We ask Jesus to be our special food and to make us strong. We will listen to Jesus, speaking silently in our hearts.

At the end of Mass, the priest blesses us in the name of the Blessed Trinity. We make the sign of the cross and then stand while the priest leaves the altar. We thank God for giving us the grace to take part in the Mass. We may sing a hymn to thank Him. We ask Him to be with us all the days of our life.

How fortunate we are to be able to offer the Holy Mass to God the Father with Jesus!

## In the Textbook

Read lesson 15.

## REINFORCEMENT

### Summary

The Mass is made up of four parts — Entrance Rite, Liturgy of the Word, Liturgy of the Eucharist, Dismissal. The most important parts are the Liturgy of the Word, in which God speaks to us through the Bible and the priest, and the Liturgy of the Eucharist, in which Jesus becomes present, offers Himself to the Father, and comes to us in Holy Communion.

### Application

"I will learn about the Mass," trying to understand what is taking place.

### Activity

*Take the children into the church and, after a reverent prayer before Jesus in the Blessed Sacrament, gather them around the altar.*

This is where Mass is celebrated. Does the altar remind you of anything you have in your own home? *Pupil response.* How is it like a table? How is it different? *Discuss.*

*Call the children's attention to:*

— the crucifix, which is always on or near the altar to remind us that in the Mass Jesus gives Himself to His Father, as He did on the cross *(familiarize the children with the word "crucifix," if necessary);*

— the candles, at least two of which are always on or near the altar to show that we are praying and celebrating.

The Mass is a celebration. People celebrate when they are happy about something good — even something that happened a long time ago. On birthdays, for example, we celebrate because we were born.

*You might wish to speak of other celebrations, too, such as the Fourth of July, wedding anniversaries, etc.* At Mass we celebrate because Jesus died and rose for us.

*Ask what the children do at a celebration in their homes. Pupil response.*

The Mass is a celebration in many ways:

Our heavenly Father invites us to come to visit Him in His house.

Jesus, our Brother, invites us to join Him as He gives Himself to God the Father. The priest stands for Jesus. We don't see Jesus, but He is there just the same.

We come together with other members of God's family. All the people at Mass are children of God our Father and brothers and sisters of Jesus.

At Mass Jesus gives Himself to us as our food — the most special food in the world!

So the Mass is a real celebration. But it is more than that. It is a very special kind of religious ceremony, because Jesus is present and leads us in our worship of the Father.

*Ask the children whether they remember the precious cups, plate and pitchers that the priest uses at Mass. How are these like ordinary dishes? How are they different? Pupil response. Lead the children to observe that these "dishes" (called vessels) are special — and special because of their purpose: at Mass the bread and wine that they contain become the body and blood of Jesus Himself.* The cruets are special pitchers. One contains water; the other, wine. The priest pours some of the wine into the chalice, and also a little water. The water becomes part of the wine. Later, of course, the wine in the chalice becomes the blood of Jesus.

The paten is a special plate. On it rests the large host that the priest holds up after the Consecration.

The chalice is a special cup. Into the chalice the priest pours wine, which becomes the blood of Jesus during the Mass.

The ciborium, too, is like a cup, but it is covered. It contains the hosts, each of which becomes the body of Christ at the Consecration.

*Talk about the special clothes the priest wears at Mass.* He wears these clothes to show that he has something special to do. He has to take the place of Jesus. *Your discussion of what the priest wears could be limited to the most conspicuous of the vestments — the chasuble. You might ask the children what colors they have seen the priest wearing and briefly explain the main liturgical colors:*

> violet — waiting and being sorry for sins
> white — joy
> red — martyrdom; descent of the Holy Spirit (both of these will need a word or two of explanation)
> green — growing in God's life; hoping for heaven

*Show the children the pulpit or lectern and explain that before Jesus gives Himself to the Father through the priest, He speaks to us, His brothers and sisters, through the Bible, God's Book. It is not necessary to burden the children with the term "lectionary." Likewise with the sacramentary; it may simply be referred to as a Mass book containing the prayers that the priest says.*

*If possible, bring the class into the sacristy where someone — perhaps one of the parish priests or a deacon — is waiting to show them the vessels and vestments you have talked about. Maintain an atmosphere of reverence.*

*N.B. If the above activity is not possible, turn to chapter 15 in the activity book and look at the pictures, or hold up posters that you have made, based on the drawings on pp. 149-153 of this manual.*

## Assignment

*Give the children as much help as they will need in order to accomplish the assignment successfully.*

## ADDITIONAL AIDS AND ACTIVITIES

### At Home or in the Classroom

**Poster Scramble.** Scramble the four posters you have made on the parts of the Mass and ask the children to arrange them correctly. If you also have the poster series on the Mass from the St. Paul Catechetical Center, explain each picture to the children. Then scramble these posters, too, and let the class put them in order.

## *At Home or in the Classroom*

**Posters To Make.** Trace these drawings to make patterns for construction-paper posters. You could design the posters yourself and use them for teaching and reviewing, or the children could make them as an aid to assimilation.

cruets

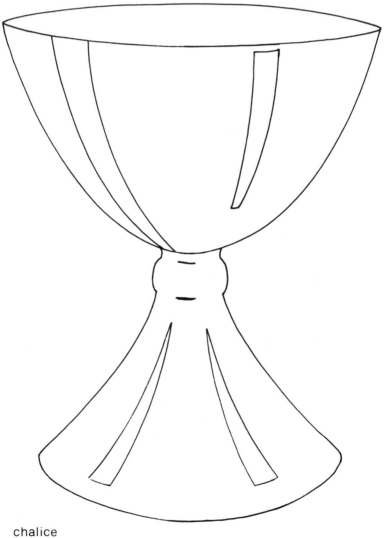

chalice

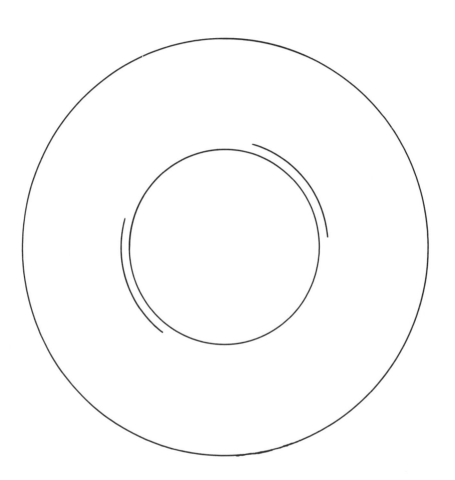

paten

ciborium

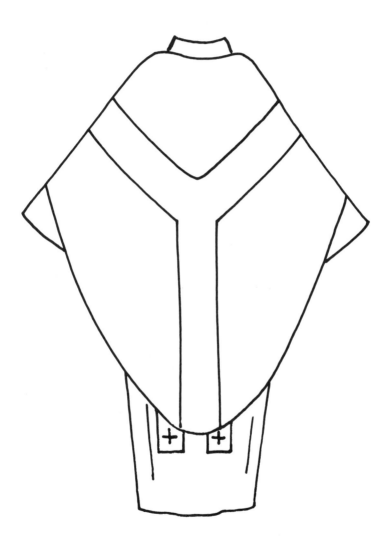

chasuble

# 16

# Why Jesus Offers
# the Mass

## TO PARENTS AND TEACHERS

This chapter is on the four main purposes for which the Mass is offered: thanksgiving, adoration or praise, atonement and petition. In the preceding chapter the children learned something about what the priest does at Mass; here, they learn something about their own role — how to unite their prayers with those of Jesus.

## TO PARENTS ESPECIALLY

There are times when a spiritual checkup is useful. Right now, as your child is learning to pray the Mass, you might like to ask yourself some questions about your own Mass participation. For example:

— Do I praise and thank God with my heart as well as with my lips?

— Do I ask God's forgiveness for myself and others?

— Am I confident that He can help me in my needs, and do I ask His help?

— Do I regard the Scriptures as God speaking to us — teaching us about Himself and about ourselves?

— Do I offer myself with my Lord in His sacrifice?

— Do I think of the Lord Jesus, present in the Eucharist, as the living heart of my parish community?

# PREPARATION

## Theme and Aim

The Mass is offered to give thanks to God, to praise Him, to ask His forgiveness and to ask His help.
"I will pray well at Mass."

## Key Word

Eucharist

## Suggested Preparatory Reading

—As soon as the Samaritan realized that he had been cleansed from leprosy, he went back to thank Jesus (Luke 17:11-16).

—Jesus gave thanks to the Father for having revealed the mystery of salvation to little ones (Luke 10:21-22).

—In heaven the blessed give glory to God (Revelation 19:1-18).

—St. Paul exhorts Christians to praise and thank the Lord (Ephesians 1:3-6; 5:20; Colossians 3:15-17).

## Materials

recording of lively music

# PRESENTATION

## Introduction

Explain to the children that today we will learn more about what the Mass means, now that they have a general understanding of the main parts.

## Message

First, I will tell you this story from God's Holy Book:
Once Jesus and His friends, the apostles, were walking along a country road. They came to a small village.

"Look there!" said one of the apostles. "Some lepers are calling to us." There near the village gate stood a group of about ten men. They looked very sad, for they had a bad skin disease called leprosy. People didn't know how to cure leprosy. The disease would become worse and worse until the men died.

"Jesus, Master!" the lepers called out. "Have pity on us!" The lepers wanted Jesus to feel sorry for them and help them. Jesus did feel sorry for them. He knew that besides being sick these men were sad because other people wouldn't go near them for fear of catching the disease.

"Go and show yourselves to the priests," said Jesus. In His country the priests had the duty of deciding whether people had leprosy or not.

The lepers started out to find a priest. While they were on their way, they realized that their skin had become just like anybody else's. They had been cured!

One of the lepers turned around and ran back to find Jesus. "May God be praised!" he shouted. "I've been cured!" He knelt down in front of Jesus. "Thank You!" he exclaimed. "What wonderful things You can do! Thank You! Thank You!"

Jesus was pleased that the man had come back to thank Him. But He was also sad. "Were not all ten cured?" He asked. Of course, He **knew** that they had been cured. "Where are the other nine?" He continued. "Wasn't there anyone else to come back and give thanks to God?"

This story has an important lesson for us. God has done so many things for us. And when someone does something for us, what should we say? *Wait for response.* Yes, we should say "thank you." What are some of the things God has done for us? (He made us. He made us His children through Baptism. He feeds us with Himself in Holy Communion. He helps us to reach heaven....)

*Discuss the Mass as a great prayer in which we can join Jesus in thanking and praising our heavenly Father. Explain the other purposes for which the Mass is offered: to ask God's forgiveness and make up for sin; to ask God's help for ourselves and others.*

## In the Textbook

*Read lesson 16.*

## REINFORCEMENT

### Summary

The Mass is offered for four main purposes: to praise God, to thank Him, to ask His forgiveness and to ask His help.

### Application

"I will pray well at Mass."

### Activity

*You might start out by playing a recording of lively music and having the class skip around the room in a circle. Then stop and talk about what we showed when we were doing this.* (Happiness.)

*Explain that there are many ways of showing what we think and feel. Perform one or two gestures familiar to the class (such as waving or holding out your hand as if expecting something to be placed in it). Ask what each gesture means. Lead the children to the concept that we can sometimes speak by what we do, without using any words.*

At Mass, too, we sometimes speak by what we do. This is one of the actions that belongs to the Mass.

*It might be well to catch the children's attention by showing them one of the less familiar gestures, such as the signing of the cross with one's thumb on forehead, lips and heart. Teach them how to do it. After they have learned how to perform the gesture correctly, explain its meaning:*

We make these three little crosses just before we listen to a reading from the most important part of the Bible, God's Book. This most important part is the Gospel. These three little crosses are like a prayer. When we make the sign of the cross on our **forehead** we show that we want to **think about** what Jesus says to us in the Gospel. When we make it on our **lips** we show that we want to **talk to others about** what Jesus says to us in the Gospel. When we make it on our **heart,** we show that we want to **love** what Jesus says to us in the Gospel. *Go over it again, helping the children to make the connection: with the head we think, with the lips we speak and with the heart we love. Drill on the gesture and its meaning for another minute or two.*

*The next gesture that you might show the children is the striking of the breast (done during the prayer "I confess...").* After they have learned how to do it, you could explain it in this way: It is the opposite of pointing our finger at someone else and saying, "He did it; it's his fault." Instead, we "point the finger" at ourselves and say, "It's my fault; I did it."

*The bow, made during the Creed, may be explained — after the children have practiced it — as a sign of respect. It is a way of adoring God.*

*Show the children how to join their hands, palms together, and how to fold them with fingers interlocked. Explain that either attitude expresses willingness to do whatever God expects of us.*

*The genuflection (with which the children should be familiar by now) is also a sign of respect, a way of adoring God. So is kneeling.*

*Ask the children to compare the height of a child who is genuflecting with that of one who is standing. Make the same comparison between kneeling and standing children.* Those who are kneeling or genuflecting look smaller. We are always small before God, because He is so great. But we genuflect or kneel to make ourselves even smaller, to show that we **know** how great God is. This is a way of adoring God.

Sometimes we sit down at Mass. In class when we sit down we might read or listen.... *Make appropriate comparisons with the children's own daily life. You could mention an educational television program that many of your students watch or an educational film you know they have seen.* At Mass, too, we sit down to **listen** and **learn.** Sometimes we also **pray** sitting down.

We **stand** at Mass to show that we are ready to do what God asks us to do. *Have the children stand up and remain standing until you reach the "Message" part of the lesson. If they acted out the first Passover, you might invite them to recall that they pretended to be eating while standing up to show that they were ready to go on a trip.* So standing shows that we are ready— ready to take part in the Mass or ready to do what Jesus teaches in the Gospel or ready to praise and thank God, *and so forth.*

The sign of the cross is made at the beginning and end of the Mass. When all of us make it together we think of Jesus' death for us and of the three wonderful Persons of the Trinity. When the priest turns toward us and makes the sign of the cross, he is asking God to help us and take care of us. We say the priest is **blessing** us. When he does this, we, too, make the sign of the cross.

*N.B. A poem summarizing our actions at Mass will be found in the activity book, on the page entitled "Poems and a Song." The children could read or recite it all together, performing the gestures as they say the words.*

## Assignment

*Explain how to do the activity book assignment.*

# ADDITIONAL AIDS AND ACTIVITIES

## At Home or in the Classroom

**Learning Mass Prayers.** Using Mass books or missalettes, start to teach the children some of the shorter and simpler Mass responses.

## At Home or in the Classroom

**Yarn "Drawings."** Show the children how to make a simple chalice pattern by folding scrap paper in half and cutting it. (See the sketch on the next page.)

Have them make a host by tracing any round object. Leaving space for a Scripture quote at the bottom, they could trace the host and chalice onto a sheet of colored construction paper and punch holes along the outline. Yarn is then woven in and out through the holes (with the knots on the same side as the pencil marks). The children should go around twice, so the host and chalice are "solidly" outlined. They might change colors on their second time around. Beneath the design the children may letter a phrase from their religion books, such as "This is my body. Take and eat," or "I am the living bread." Another appropriate quote is, "I am the bread of life" (Jn. 6:48). These drawings may be taken home to be hung up as a reminder of (the approaching day of) first Communion.

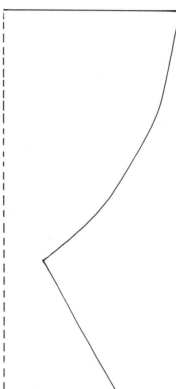

# 17
# At Mass We Listen to God's Word

## TO PARENTS AND TEACHERS

This chapter is about the first part of the Mass, the Liturgy of the Word. The importance of God's Word could be stressed by pointing out that it is read in every Mass and in the sacrament of Penance. The children should also be helped to appreciate the dialogue nature of the Liturgy of the Word: God speaks to us and we to Him.

## TO PARENTS ESPECIALLY

Obtain a Bible, if you do not already have one, and give it a place of honor in your home.

## PREPARATION

### Theme and Aim

At Mass God speaks to us, His people, through the Bible. We answer Him in prayer.
"I will obey God's Word."

### Key Words

agreement              homily
Word of God            creed
readings

## Suggested Preparatory Reading

—*The Word of God is food for the soul (Matthew 4:4; Constitution on Divine Revelation, n. 21).*

—*The Word of God is always fruitful (Isaiah 55:10-11; Hebrews 4:12). It is efficacious in proportion to our interior response (1 Samuel 3).*

—*It is not enough to hear the Word of God; it must be put into practice (Matthew 7:24; 15:8; 28:20).*

—*The Church, in her Liturgy, manifests her faith in the presence of the Lord in the Scriptures by incensing the Sacred Book; by asking for purification of heart and lips with the prayer "Cleanse my heart and my lips..." to worthily proclaim it; and by kissing the sacred text at the end of the reading as a sign of veneration (cf. Order of Mass).*

—*The Lord is present in His Word, since it is He Himself who speaks when the holy Scriptures are read in the church (Constitution on the Sacred Liturgy, no. 7).*

## Materials

Bible (illustrated, if possible)

Mass booklets (such as St. Paul Mass Book for Children)

*optional*—

homemade charts summarizing the Liturgy of the Word

# PRESENTATION

## Introduction

*Spontaneous prayer.*

*After going over the activity book work together, hold up the classroom Bible. Ask the children what it is. Speak of it as God's Holy Book—the letter that our loving Father has written to us. Show some of the pictures and explain that each of the stories in the Bible has something to teach us.*

The Bible is read during the first part of the Mass. Today we will learn about this part of the Mass.

## *Message*

*There are two ways in which this lesson could be presented. If it isn't feasible to make the cards, the class could go through the structure of the Mass using only the Mass booklets, while you give an explanation based on the suggestions that have been given here for the cards. It would be well to keep the class members involved by having them perform the gestures and take the proper positions. Asking questions would also be helpful. Suggestions for these are provided here.*

### Entrance Rite

*All stand. Ask the children the purpose of standing —* What do we "say" to God and other people by standing? (We are ready to do what God wishes us to do.)

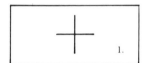

| | |
|---|---|
| (cross) 1. | WE MAKE THE SIGN OF THE CROSS WITH THE PRIEST. 1. |

*Ask the meaning of the sign of the cross.*

| | |
|---|---|
| THE PRIEST ASKS GOD TO BE CLOSE TO US. HE SAYS: "THE LORD BE WITH YOU." 2. | WE ASK GOD TO BE CLOSE TO THE PRIEST. USUALLY WE SAY: "AND ALSO WITH YOU." 2. |
| THE PRIEST ASKS US TO REMEMBER OUR SINS. 3. | WE THINK ABOUT OUR SINS AND FAULTS, WHICH HAVE DISPLEASED OUR LOVING FATHER. 3. |

WE SAY PRAYERS
ASKING GOD TO
FORGIVE US.
4.

Show the children these penitential prayers in the Mass booklet, at the same time reviewing the gesture of striking one's breast and its meaning.

PRIEST AND PEOPLE:
"GLORY TO GOD IN
THE HIGHEST...."
5.

WE SAY A LONG,
BEAUTIFUL PRAYER
THAT PRAISES GOD THE
FATHER AND JESUS HIS
SON, WITH THE
HOLY SPIRIT.
5.

THE PRIEST SAYS:
"LET US PRAY."
THEN HE SAYS A
PRAYER.
6.

IN OUR HEARTS WE ASK
GOD TO HELP US AND
OTHERS. AFTER THE
PRIEST PRAYS, WE
ANSWER: "AMEN."
6.

Ask whether anyone knows the meaning of "Amen" — "I really mean it."

### Liturgy of the Word

Display the homemade Liturgy of the Word poster, so the children will understand what part of the Mass they are about to study.

Then invite the class to sit, and ask the children the meaning of sitting down during the Mass.

FIRST READING
"...THIS IS THE WORD
OF THE LORD."
7.

GOD SPEAKS TO US
THROUGH HIS BOOK,
THE BIBLE.
THEN WE SAY: "THANKS
BE TO GOD."
7.

*You might wish·to explain that "Thanks be to God"*
*means "Thank You, God—thank You for speaking to us."*

| | |
|---|---|
| RESPONSORIAL<br>PSALM<br><div align="right">8.</div> | WE TAKE TURNS WITH<br>THE READER IN SAYING<br>A PRAYER FROM THE<br>BIBLE.<br><div align="right">8.</div> |
| SECOND READING<br>"...THIS IS THE WORD<br>OF THE LORD."<br><div align="right">9.</div> | GOD SPEAKS TO US<br>AGAIN THROUGH HIS<br>BOOK, THE BIBLE.<br>THEN WE SAY:<br>"THANKS BE TO GOD."<br><div align="right">9.</div> |

*You might review the meaning of "Thanks be to God,"*
*which you have just treated.*
*Stand, and again review the purpose of standing*
*during Mass.*

| | |
|---|---|
| A SHORT PRAYER.<br>USUALLY IT STARTS<br>WITH<br>"ALLELUIA."<br><div align="right">10.</div> | WE REPEAT THE<br>BEGINNING OF THE<br>PRAYER.<br><div align="right">10.</div> |

*Ask whether the children remember the meaning of*
*"Alleluia." ("Let's praise God.")*

| | |
|---|---|
| THE PRIEST SAYS:<br>"THE LORD BE WITH<br>YOU."<br><div align="right">11.</div> | WE ANSWER:<br>"AND ALSO WITH<br>YOU."<br><div align="right">11.</div> |

*Review the meaning of these expressions.* (The priest asks God to be close to us and we ask God to be close to the priest.)

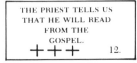

*Tell the children that this is the point at which to make the three small crosses on forehead, lips and heart. Review the purpose of these small crosses—to think about God's Word, to tell others about it and to love it.*

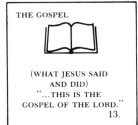

*Then all are seated.*

| THE HOMILY. THE PRIEST TELLS US WHAT WE SHOULD BELIEVE AND DO. 14. | IN OUR HEARTS WE PROMISE JESUS THAT WE WILL DO WHATEVER THE PRIEST TELLS US. 14. |

*All stand.*

| THE CREED, ALSO CALLED THE PROCLAMATION OF FAITH. 15. | WE SAY THIS LONG PRAYER TO TELL GOD THAT WE BELIEVE EVERYTHING HE HAS TAUGHT US. 15. |

| | |
|---|---|
| THE PRAYER OF THE FAITHFUL (ALSO CALLED THE GENERAL INTERCESSIONS). 16. | WE PRAY FOR EVERYONE BY ANSWERING: ° 16. |

*On your own homemade card fill in the response usually used in your own parish, such as, "Lord, hear our prayer."

## In the Textbook

Read lesson 17.

# REINFORCEMENT

## Summary

At Mass God speaks to us through the readings from His Word and the priest's homily. We answer Him by saying the Creed.

## Application

"I will obey God's Word."

## Activity

Teach the children part of the "Song about Mass" that they will find in their activity books (under the section "for chapters 15-19"). The music is available on cassette from the St. Paul Catechetical Center. The first six verses of this song sum up the Liturgy of the Word.

## Assignment

Show the children what to do in their activity books.

## ADDITIONAL AIDS AND ACTIVITIES

### At Home

**Mass Preparation.** Before Mass — perhaps even in the car on the way to church — explain the Sunday readings to your child.

### At Home

**Weekly discussion.** Form the custom of holding a brief, mealtime discussion of the Sunday homily. Try to have each member suggest a practical application of the homily to his daily life.

### At Home or in the Classroom

**Responsorial Prayer.** The children might learn "O God, I Am Looking for You," based on Psalm 63. It will be found in the activity book, under the heading: "for chapters 15-22."

*Leader:* O God, I am looking for You.
*Class:*  O God, I am looking for You.
*Leader:* For You, O God, I am thirsty, like the earth without water.
*Class:*  O God, I am looking for You.
*Leader:* I have looked toward Your holy place, to see Your power and Your glory.
*Class:*  O God, I am looking for You.
*Leader:* Your kindness is more important than life itself; I will praise You.
*Class:*  O God, I am looking for You.
*Leader:* All my life I will praise You and pray to You.
*Class:*  O God, I am looking for You.
*Leader:* As in a special meal, You will fill my soul, and I will praise You.
*Class:*  O God, I am looking for You.
*Pause.*

*Leader:* Now let us tell Jesus in the silence of our hearts how happy we are that He gave us a share in His own life in Baptism, comes to forgive our sins in Penance and will soon strengthen us with His own body and blood in Communion. *Silent prayer.*

# 18
# With Jesus We Offer Ourselves to the Father

## TO PARENTS AND TEACHERS

This lesson concentrates on the very heart of the Mass — the sacrifice of Jesus, renewed on the altar for our good and that of the world in which we live. The children should be taught reverence for the Mystery of Faith, in which Jesus becomes truly present and offers His sacrifice again. An attitude of prayerful silence during and after the solemn moment of the Consecration is to be encouraged.

## PREPARATION

### Theme and Aim

Jesus gave His life for us and renews this offering in every Mass.

"I will give my special offering at Mass."

### Key Word

Consecration

### Suggested Preparatory Reading

**FROM THE GENERAL CATECHETICAL DIRECTORY:**

"The primacy of the Eucharist over all the other sacraments is unquestionable, as is also its supreme efficacy in building up the Church.

"For in the Eucharist, when the words of consecration have been pronounced, the profound (not the
phenomenal) reality of bread and wine is changed into
the body and blood of Christ, and this wonderful change
has in the Church come to be called 'transubstantiation.'
Accordingly, under the appearances (that is, the phenomenal reality) of the bread and wine, the humanity of Christ,
not only by its power but by itself (that is, substantially)
united with His divine Person, lies hidden in an altogether
mysterious way.

"This sacrifice is not merely a rite commemorating
a past sacrifice. For in it Christ by the ministry of the
priests perpetuates the sacrifice of the cross in an unbloody manner through the course of the centuries.
In it too He nourishes the faithful with Himself, the Bread
of Life, in order that, filled with love of God and neighbor,
they may become more and more a people acceptable
to God."

**FURTHER READINGS**

*—Abel (Genesis 4:2-5), Abraham (Genesis 22:1-19)
and Melchisedech (Genesis 14:17-20), offered pleasing
sacrifices to God; the Church recalls these sacrifices and
prays that God will gladly accept the sacrifice of the Mass.*

*—The faithful, through the hands of the priest, unite
and offer themselves together with the spotless victim
(Constitution on the Sacred Liturgy, n. 48; Constitution
on the Church, n. 11; Decree on the Ministry and Life
of Priests, n. 5).*

*—The works, prayers, labors, various difficulties and
sufferings of this life become pleasing sacrifices to God
through Jesus Christ. In the Eucharistic Celebration they
are offered to the Father with the offering of our Lord's
body (Constitution on the Church, n. 34).*

## Materials

Mass vessels and vestments or pictures of them
children's Mass books
everything suggested for the paraliturgy

*optional —*
Mass charts

# PRESENTATION

## Introduction

*Our Father.*
*After asking questions based on the activity book work, it would be well to show the sacred vessels and a chasuble (or pictures of the same) one by one and review what the children know about them.*

Today we will talk about the part of the Mass during which Jesus becomes present *(pointing)* on the paten, in the ciborium, in the chalice.

## Message

*Display the poster on the Liturgy of the Eucharist. Invite the children to sit, if they were not already seated, and ask them to imagine this part of the Mass taking place.*

PEOPLE BRING BREAD
AND WINE TO THE
ALTAR. THEY BRING
THEM FOR ALL OF US.
17.

WE USUALLY GIVE
MONEY NOW, TOO.
17.

*Talk about this. Who brings the bread and wine to the altar in your parish? Why do people give money to the Church?*

THE PRIEST OFFERS THE
BREAD AND WINE TO
GOD, OUR FATHER.
18.

WE SING A HYMN OR
ANSWER THE PRIEST:
"BLESSED BE GOD
FOR EVER."
18.

The hymn tells God that we are giving Him gifts. The little prayer has the same meaning as the Glory to the Father.

| | |
|---|---|
| THE PRIEST PRAYS THAT OUR FATHER WILL BE PLEASED WITH THIS MASS — OUR SACRIFICE. 19. | WE SAY A PRAYER THAT MEANS THE SAME AS THE PRIEST'S PRAYER. 19. |

*The children could be shown this prayer in their Mass books. All stand.*

| | |
|---|---|
| THE PRIEST SAYS A PRAYER CALLED THE "PRAYER OVER THE GIFTS." 20. | WE JOIN THE PRIEST BY ANSWERING "AMEN." 20. |

*You might wish to ask again what "Amen" means.*

| | |
|---|---|
| THE PRIEST PRAYS: "THE LORD BE WITH YOU." 21. | WE ANSWER: "AND ALSO WITH YOU." 21. |

| | |
|---|---|
| "LIFT UP YOUR HEARTS." 22. | "WE LIFT THEM UP TO THE LORD." 22. |

| | |
|---|---|
| "LET US GIVE THANKS TO THE LORD OUR GOD." 23. | "IT IS RIGHT TO GIVE HIM THANKS AND PRAISE." 23. |

| | |
|---|---|
| THE PRIEST SAYS A PRAYER OF THANKS AND PRAISE. 24. | WE FINISH THE PRAYER: "HOLY, HOLY, HOLY...." 24. |

Read the rest of this prayer in the St. Paul Mass Book for Children.

All kneel. Review the purpose of kneeling. Explain the importance of this part of the Mass, in which Jesus Himself becomes present and offers His sacrifice again.

| | |
|---|---|
| THE PRIEST PRAYS THAT THE BREAD AND WINE WILL BECOME THE BODY AND BLOOD OF JESUS CHRIST. 25. | WE LISTEN CAREFULLY. THE HOLIEST PART OF THE MASS IS COMING NOW. 25. |

Key word: **consecration**

| | |
|---|---|
| THE PRIEST SPEAKS FOR JESUS. HE SAYS: "THIS IS MY BODY.... THIS IS MY BLOOD...." 26. | WE ADORE THE HOST. THE HOST IS NOW JESUS. WE ADORE JESUS IN THE CHALICE, TOO. 26. |

You might suggest that when looking up at the elevated Host, the children could say a brief silent prayer, perhaps one of these:
— Jesus, I adore You.
— Jesus, I love You.
— My Lord and my God.
— My God and my all.
At the elevation of the chalice, they might pray:
My Jesus, mercy.
You could also suggest that the children bow their heads after each elevation as a sign of adoration.

| | |
|---|---|
| THE PRIEST SAYS: "LET US PROCLAIM THE MYSTERY OF FAITH." 27. | WE SAY A PRAYER THAT REMINDS US OF JESUS' DEATH AND RESURRECTION. 27. |

*An example of such a prayer is: "Christ has died. Christ is risen. Christ will come again."*

*Stress the fact that at this point of the Mass Jesus offers Himself to the Father—He gives Himself for us. We should tell the Father—in our hearts—that we are offering Jesus and ourselves along with Him.*

| | |
|---|---|
| THE PRIEST OFFERS JESUS TO THE FATHER FOR US AND FOR ALL THE PEOPLE OF THE WORLD.    28. | WE PRAY IN OUR HEARTS, OFFERING JESUS TO THE FATHER. WE OFFER OURSELVES, TOO, WITH JESUS.    28. |
| THE PRIEST LIFTS UP THE HOST AND CHALICE AND SAYS A PRAYER PRAISING GOD.    29. | WE JOIN IN THE PRIEST'S PRAYER BY SAYING OR SINGING "AMEN."    29. |

## Optional—Further Explanation

The Holy Eucharist is the greatest sacrament, because the Eucharist is Jesus Himself.

The Eucharist is a sacrament and a sacrifice. A sacrament is a special meeting with Jesus. who gives us grace even though we don't see Him. But what is a sacrifice? We shall see.

Before Jesus came, our heavenly Father told His People to worship Him by offering gifts such as bread, wine, oil, lambs, goats, and pigeons. These gifts were called sacrifices.

When God's People offered animals, they killed them first. They did this to show that they recognized God as the Creator and Ruler of their lives and of all they had. They also meant to tell God that they were sorry for their sins, and that their lives were His.

God's People offered sacrifices every morning and evening. On special celebrations, they offered sacrifices of **hundreds** of animals.

The sacrifices of God's People were to last only until Jesus would offer His life to our heavenly Father as a perfect sacrifice for the sins of the world. In His Holy Book, God said that we, the **new** People of God, would offer Him the sacrifice of our Savior.

As we know, during the Last Supper, Jesus took bread, blessed it, broke it and gave it to His apostles, saying, "Take this and eat it...**this is my body.**" Then Jesus took a cup of wine, gave thanks to His heavenly Father, and gave it to His apostles, saying, "All of you must drink from it...for **this is my blood,** the blood of the covenant, to be poured out in behalf of many for the forgiveness of sins" (Matthew 26:26-28).

At Jesus' words, the bread and wine really became His body and blood. Jesus offered them in sacrifice to His Father. This same body and blood were to be separated in death the very next day, Good Friday.

On Good Friday Jesus died on the cross to make up for our sins and win back for us the right to heaven. He wanted us always to remember how much He loved us. He wanted us to share in His offering to God. And He wanted to come to each of us to make us stronger in spirit and join us to one another. That is why He gave us the holy Mass.

At Mass Jesus offers Himself to the Father, as He did on the cross. At Mass we remember the death and resurrection of Jesus. At Mass, we have a special holy meal, like the Last Supper.

At the Last Supper, Jesus made His apostles **priests** and gave them the power to repeat what He had done. He gave them the power to change bread and wine into His own body and blood and to offer them in sacrifice to our heavenly Father.

The only difference between the Mass and Jesus' death on the cross is this:

On the cross, Jesus freely offered His own life to the Father and died, shedding all His blood;

In the Mass, Jesus, now risen and glorious, offers Himself again and again through His priest, in an unbloody (not bloody) way, under the appearances of bread and wine.

At the Consecration, when the priest repeats the words Jesus said at the Last Supper,

"THIS IS MY BODY"
and
"THIS IS THE CUP OF MY BLOOD,"

Jesus changes bread and wine into His own body and blood. He offers Himself to our heavenly Father for us, as He did on the cross.

Jesus prays: "Heavenly Father, I offer You again my body and blood as I did on the cross: to adore You who are so great and so good; to thank You for all the blessings You give Your children; to beg You to forgive sinners and to ask You to give Your graces to all Your people."

At this great moment we offer ourselves with Jesus to our heavenly Father and promise Him love and obedience.

We offer our whole selves, our good deeds, our joys and our sacrifices, things like obeying our parents and doing our schoolwork, even when we find it hard. We join them all to the perfect offering of Jesus Master and pray:

"Through him, with him, in him, in the unity of the Holy Spirit, all glory and honor is yours, almighty Father, for ever and ever. Amen."

How many graces we receive at Mass!... If God is so patient with our world so full of sin, it is because Mass is always being celebrated throughout the whole world, and in the Mass Jesus Himself begs our heavenly Father to forgive us our sins.

Yes, the celebration of holy Mass is the greatest and most important action that takes place anywhere. No wonder the People of God go to Mass even if they have to walk a long way or do something else difficult in order to get there. *This point could be emphasized.*

## In the Textbook

*Read lesson 18.*

# REINFORCEMENT

## Summary

In every Mass Jesus becomes present at the Consecration and renews the offering of His life for us.

## Application

"I will give my special offering at Mass." *Encourage each child to think of something special to offer to God — giving up something he likes, doing something hard to please someone else, etc.*

## Activity

*This brief paraliturgy stresses our role as co-offerers with Christ. Parts should be assigned and explained beforehand. That of the commentator may be taken by a helper; otherwise, the teacher may act as commentator.* to be prepared: *a table, an altar cloth, a crucifix, two candles, two vases of flowers, a ciborium, cruets containing water and wine, hosts, slides or posters on the Mass.*
*All stand.*
*Commentator:* We are gathered here to remember what Jesus did for us at the Last Supper and on the cross — what He continues to do every day in every Mass.
We will not be celebrating a real Mass, because only a priest can do that, but we will think about the great gift of the Mass and we will pray.
*The class is seated while two children spread the cloth on the table which stands for an altar.*
*An appropriate hymn or song is sung.*
*One of the children places the crucifix on the "altar" while the commentator explains:*
*Commentator:* There is always a crucifix on or near the altar. It reminds us that the Mass is the sacrifice of Jesus.
*Two children bring the vases of flowers and place them near the "altar."*

*Commentator:* The flowers tell us that Jesus' offering
is a joyful one. They also stand for our love for God.

*Two other children bring the candles, already lighted.*

*Commentator:* The burning candles remind us that Jesus
rose from the dead. He is the light of the world. They
also show that we are praying and celebrating.

*Another hymn or song.*

*All stand.*

*Commentator:* Now we place our hosts in the ciborium.

*The children do so, following the teacher's example.*
This little offering stands for our work, our study,
our sacrifices, joys, sorrows, and very selves.

Making this offering, we show the Father that we
want to be His, that we wish to give ourselves completely to Him as Jesus did.

*An offertory hymn is sung.*

*Two children bring cruets of wine and water to the altar;
a third carries the ciborium.*

*Commentator:* At the Last Supper, Jesus offered Himself
to the Father.

*A picture of the Last Supper is shown to the class. Mean-
while the teacher reads Luke 22:14-20.*

*The crucifix is held up.*

*Commentator:* Jesus offered Himself to make up for our
sins. And at every Mass He gives Himself to the Father again. He gives Himself for us. And the Father
accepts Jesus' offering and sacrifice. Jesus joins our
little offering to His. For this reason our gift is pleasing
to God the Father.

*Show — if possible — a picture of a priest offering the body
and blood of Christ to the Father (doxology at the
end of the Eucharistic Prayer).*
In the Mass, while the priest offers the great gift,
Jesus, to the Father, he prays to God. We listen to
his prayer and at the end we join ourselves to Jesus
by answering: Amen.

*Commentator:* Through him, with him, in him in the unity
of the Holy Spirit, all glory and honor is yours almighty Father, for ever and ever.

*Class:* Amen.
*The celebration concludes with another Eucharistic song or hymn.*

## Assignment

*See "application" on p. 177.*

## ADDITIONAL AIDS AND ACTIVITIES

## As a Family

**Silent prayer.** Each Sunday (Saturday evening) go to church a little before Mass begins, so as to have time to reflect on the readings beforehand and silently offer the Lord all the joys and sorrows, studies and work of the coming week.

# 19
# God the Father
# Gives Us Jesus

## TO PARENTS AND TEACHERS

The completion of the Mass is Holy Communion, for our Eucharistic Savior has chosen to come to us as our spiritual food. Help the children to appreciate the importance of this nourishment in our struggle to overcome selfishness and temptations, in our efforts to become more like Jesus.

Penance and Eucharist are always to be viewed as two of the greatest means of growing in Christ.

## TO PARENTS ESPECIALLY

Children are likely to be most attentive during those moments of the Mass when they are most active — for example, when singing, contributing to the collection, taking part in the offertory procession, exchanging the sign of peace, or filing up to receive Communion. Hence, the need to stress their role during more silent moments — reflection on God's Word to make it a part of life, the offering of oneself to the Father with Jesus in the greatest of all acts of worship, heart-to-heart conversation with our Savior after having received Him or whenever one pays a visit to the Blessed Sacrament.

Your own example will be the greatest incentive to your boy or girl for living a truly Eucharistic life.

# PREPARATION

## Theme and Aim

At Communion, God the Father gives us Jesus as the Bread of Life. Jesus gives us more grace and strength. He makes us more like Himself and promises us heaven.

"I will be happy to receive Jesus."

## Key Word

everlasting

## Suggested Preparatory Reading

**FROM THE INSTRUCTION ON WORSHIP OF THE EUCHARISTIC MYSTERY:**

"Everyone who has participated in the Mass should be eager to do good works, to please God and to live honestly, devoted to the Church, putting into practice what he has learned, and growing in piety. He will seek to fill the world with the Spirit of Christ and in all things, in the very midst of human affairs, to become a witness of Christ" (n. 13).

**SCRIPTURE PASSAGES FOR REFLECTION:**

— *The Eucharist is necessary for spiritual life, as bread is for material life (John 6:32-35).*

— *Manna was the nourishment for the people of Israel as they wandered through the desert (Exodus 16).*

— *Christ is the true manna which nourishes the new People of God (John 6:26-58).*

— *Jesus broke bread with the disciples of Emmaus (Luke 24:30).*

— *The breaking of bread united the first Christians (Acts 2:42ff.; 20:7ff.).*

## Materials

Mass posters and charts
Mass books
everything needed in preparation for the special Mass (see p. 188)

## PRESENTATION

### Introduction

*Our Father.*
*The children might be invited to think back over the week and remember whether they really did something to offer to Jesus at Mass. Ask them not to say it out loud, however.*

If you forgot this week, try to remember to do it next week. It would be good to do something **every** week.

*Be careful, however, not to make the children scrupulous.*

*The new lesson could be introduced with the following story:*

A boy who had just made his first holy Communion was given a beautiful crucifix on a chain. A priest asked him, "What is the difference between Jesus here on the cross you are wearing and Jesus in the Eucharist whom you received this morning?"

That boy knew the answer right away!

What do you think he said? *Wait for response.*

That boy said, "Here we see a picture of Jesus, but He isn't really here! In Communion, instead, we can't see Jesus, but He's really there!"

Wasn't that a good answer?

### Message

Today we will talk about the second part of the Liturgy of the Eucharist *(display the "Liturgy of the Eucharist" poster).* This is the Communion part.

*All stand.*

| | |
|---|---|
| THE PRIEST INVITES US TO PRAY THE OUR FATHER. <br> 30. | WE SAY THE OUR FATHER, THE PRAYER THAT JESUS TAUGHT US. <br> 30. |

THE PRIEST ASKS
GOD TO KEEP US
SAFE AND HAPPY.
31.

WE ADD TO HIS
PRAYER BY SAYING
THAT GOD CAN DO
ALL THINGS.
31.

*Read the prayer to them:* "For the kingdom, the power, and the glory are yours, now and for ever." *This is another prayer of praise to God.*

THE PRIEST PRAYS:
"THE PEACE OF THE
LORD BE WITH YOU
ALWAYS."
32.

WE ANSWER:
"AND ALSO
WITH YOU."
32.

WE EXCHANGE
A SIGN OF PEACE.
THIS MEANS WE
SHOW THAT WE ARE
FRIENDS.
33.

*Probably the children are familiar with this gesture. Have them exchange the sign of peace now.*

WE PRAY TO JESUS,
WHO IS SOMETIMES
CALLED THE LAMB
OF GOD. WE ASK
FOR HIS FORGIVENESS
AND PEACE.
34.

WE PRAY:
"LAMB OF GOD,
YOU TAKE AWAY
THE SINS OF THE
WORLD: HAVE
MERCY ON US."
34.

*Ask why Jesus is called the Lamb of God.* (He offered Himself to the Father in sacrifice the way people used to offer lambs.) *Explain that we say the prayer twice in the way it is here and that the third time we replace "have mercy on us" with "grant us peace."*

| | |
|---|---|
| THE PRIEST SHOWS US THE BODY OF JESUS AND PRAYS: "...HAPPY ARE THOSE WHO ARE CALLED TO HIS SUPPER." | WE PRAY: "LORD, I AM NOT WORTHY TO RECEIVE YOU, BUT ONLY SAY THE WORD, AND I SHALL BE HEALED." 35. |

GOD'S PEOPLE
GO UP TO
RECEIVE
COMMUNION.
36.

*Explain the way one should go up (with folded hands, singing or praying silently).*

| | |
|---|---|
| THE PRIEST SAYS: "THE BODY OF CHRIST." | WE ANSWER: "AMEN." 37. |

*Explain the meaning of this particular "Amen" — "Yes, I know that this is the body of Christ."*

WE COME BACK
FROM COMMUNION
AND TALK WITH
JESUS IN OUR
HEARTS.
38.

*This might be a good time to explain what we can tell Jesus. We can thank Him for coming to us. We can tell Him that we love Him. We can ask Him to help us, to take care of us, and to make His life grow in us. We can pray for our families and friends and all the people in the world.*

| | |
|---|---|
| THE PRIEST SAYS A PRAYER CALLED THE "PRAYER AFTER COMMUNION." 39. | WE JOIN THE PRIEST BY ANSWERING: "AMEN." 39. |

*Dismissal*
*Put up the "dismissal" poster.*

| | |
|---|---|
| THE PRIEST PRAYS:<br>"THE LORD BE<br>WITH YOU." 40. | WE ANSWER:<br>"AND ALSO<br>WITH YOU." 40. |
| THE PRIEST GIVES<br>US GOD'S BLESSING.<br>41. | WE ANSWER:<br>"AMEN."<br>41. |
| THE PRIEST TELLS US<br>THAT MASS IS OVER.<br>42. | WE THANK GOD FOR<br>THE MASS<br>BY SAYING:<br>"THANKS BE TO GOD."<br>42. |

## *In the Textbook*

*Read chapter 19.*

## REINFORCEMENT

## *Summary*

At Communion, God the Father gives us Jesus as the Bread of Life. Jesus gives us more grace and strength. He makes us more like Himself and promises us heaven (of course, to go to heaven, we must live as God's good children).

## *Application*

"I will be happy to receive Jesus." *Encourage the children to look forward to first Communion. Do not, however, lead them to expect too much. The Lord may or may not choose to make His presence really* felt.

## Activity

It is to be hoped that the children will soon have a chance to take part in a Mass or paraliturgy celebrated especially for them. (See pp. 188ff.)

The class could now be divided into groups ("committees"), one to plan out what hymns and songs will be sung (see the suggestions on pp. 188-189), another to decide upon and make decorations for the church or classroom, a third to choose which explanations from the cards will be read as commentary at various points. If time does not permit much preparation at this point, the decorations may be completed at home while the teacher and/or other adults type up and run off mimeographed booklets containing the hymns, commentary and any other parts in which the children will be involved.

## Assignment

Chapter 19 in the activity book.

## ADDITIONAL AIDS AND ACTIVITIES

### In the Classroom

**Drill with the Cards.** The cards are divided into three groups, according to the lessons in which they were used. Likewise, divide the class into three groups and ask the children in each team to put their cards in order by number, look at the order carefully, and then copy the numbers onto the backs of the cards, covering those on front with masking tape. The cards are then scrambled and the children practice putting them in order, checking themselves after each attempt. When all are proficient, the groups can rotate.

### At Home or in the Classroom

**Active Drill.** Using the numbered cards and Mass books, the class could practice what we say and do at

Mass. You might wish to leave aside the longer prayers and concentrate on brief responses.

## At Home or in the Classroom

**Learning by Copying.** Using ruled paper, to be tied or stapled together afterwards, the children may make booklets of the shorter Mass responses. These could be divided into the following sections:

Entrance Rite
Liturgy of the Word
Liturgy of the Eucharist
Dismissal

# A Mass for Our Class

*Introductory Note:*

It is suggested that this Mass be offered two or three weeks before the children's first reception of the Eucharist. This kind of Mass would be one of the special ones for children. If it is not possible to have an actual Mass, a paraliturgy may be held instead.

The children should have as much participation as possible in this celebration of the Eucharist. For example, they may enter the church in procession, carrying banners or posters they have made themselves. If simple readings are chosen, the children may act as lectors and also lead the responsorial psalm. Many or all of the class members could offer petitions during the Prayer of the Faithful. During the offertory they may bring up the cruets and ciborium, as well as other gifts, such as banners, hand-written prayers, resolutions, presents for the poor.... They might also dialogue with the priest during the homily, he asking questions and they answering.

The children have learned several hymns and songs appropriate for the Eucharistic Celebration, such as: "Jesus, We Believe," and "Bread and Wine." From the "Children Sing!" cassette, they could also learn "God Within Us" and "What Do I Have To Offer My Lord?" Other hymns or songs suitable for them to learn are:

If the Mass is to be held in someone's home, the children could have a hand in preparing a centerpiece, place mats and other decorations for a get-together that will follow the celebration of the liturgy.

The commentary suggestions given here could be amplified or changed to fit the needs of the class. For example, you might prefer to replace them with some of the brief explanations that have already been presented to the children on the cards. Or, if the children have time to prepare well, they themselves might take turns in giving simple commentaries.

## The Mass

*It would be fitting for the children to use Mass books, missalettes, or response leaflets. The adults present should recite the people's parts slowly and clearly, so that the children may join in.*

*After the greeting, the priest introduces the Mass of the day with these or similar words:*

The Lord Jesus has invited us here to celebrate His sacrifice with Him, just as He invited His apostles to the Last Supper. The color used in today's Mass is................. because....................... The Mass is a wonderful and holy celebration, so we will prepare for it by telling God and our brothers how sorry we are for everything wrong we have done....

*After the Penitential Rite, if the Gloria is said or sung, the commentator introduces it as a hymn of praise.*

## Liturgy of the Word

*Commentator:* God will let us hear His own words through the readings from His Holy Book, the Bible, and through the little talk the priest will give. Let us be ready to listen to the voice of God.

*The commentator may point out the following: In the homily the priest explains the Word of God to us. In the Creed, said on the more solemn days, such as Sunday, we say that we believe everything God has taught us. In the Prayer of the Faithful we pray to God for ourselves and for other people who need God's help.*

## Liturgy of the Eucharist

*Commentator:* Now the sacrifice part of the Mass is beginning. We will bring our gifts of bread and wine to the altar.

*At this point the children prepare to bring the water, wine, hosts and perhaps other gifts to the altar. If gifts for the poor are brought, the commentator may say that they are "our offerings for our brothers in Christ." Before the offering of the gifts by the priest takes place, a hymn may be sung.*

*Commentator:* Our gifts are now on the altar. Let us watch what the priest is doing. *Pause.*

He takes the paten with the bread in his hands and lifting it toward heaven, gives thanks to God the Father. *Pause.*

Now he takes the cup containing wine and, raising it toward heaven, again gives thanks to the Father.

*Immediately after the Prayer over the Gifts, the commentator introduces the Eucharistic Prayer.*

*Commentator:* The priest will now say the great prayer of praise and thanksgiving to God. The most important and holy moment of the Mass is going to begin. Let us join with the priest to thank and praise God for all the gifts He gives us.

*Before the Consecration, the priest pauses so that the commentator may explain what is about to happen.*

*Commentator:* Let us pay attention to what the priest will do now. He will repeat the words and actions of Jesus at the Last Supper. He will take bread and say: "This is my body." He will take the cup and say: "This is my blood."
*After the Consecration, before the Memorial Acclamation:*

*Commentator:* Now Jesus is among us. Let us adore Him and say that He died and rose for us....

*After the Memorial Acclamation:*
*Commentator:* As the Mass continues, let us offer Jesus to the Father and ourselves with Him. Let us offer our work and play, our joys, our obedience, our little sacrifices....

*Before the doxology that closes the Eucharistic Prayer:*
*Commentator:* Now the priest takes the body and blood of Jesus and lifts them toward heaven to offer them to God the Father. We renew our own offering by answering: Amen.

*After the doxology:*
*Commentator:* The Lord Jesus is here with us and wants to come to His friends. Anyone who goes to Communion should have love for his neighbor. Let us pray for this love by saying the Our Father.

*Before the Sign of Peace:*
*Commentator:* We are all brothers. With the sign of peace we show that we all love one another as the Lord Jesus wants us to. *Here the commentator mentions the handshake or other local custom which constitutes the sign of peace.*

*At Communion time:*
*Commentator:* Jesus' friends will go up to receive Him in Holy Communion. You, too, would like to receive Him, and soon you will. Tell Jesus that you are looking forward to the day of your first Communion.

*After Communion:*

*Commentator:* Let us pray to the Lord Jesus. Let us adore Him. Let us thank Him for all His gifts to us. Let us tell Him we want to be His close friends always. Let us tell Him we want to live as He wishes us to live. Let us tell Him we want to love all men, our brothers.

**Concluding Rite**

*Commentator:* Before we leave the church, our risen Lord, Jesus Christ, gives us His blessing through the priest.

# 20
# How We Receive Jesus

## TO PARENTS AND TEACHERS

This is a practical lesson. The children are to learn what they must do in order to receive Communion worthily and properly. Young though they are, they should be taught about the necessity of freedom from mortal sin, for later they may need to know this. They should also be taught to go without food (or drink) for an hour before Communion. (It is well to come down to such particulars as chewing gum!) Water and medicine do not break the fast.

The **way** to receive Communion is spelled out in the activity section at the end of this lesson.

## TO PARENTS ESPECIALLY

First Communion is not so much a goal as a beginning. Hence, exterior celebrating should not be over-emphasized, lest the child think that only **this** Communion is important. (It is not uncommon for older children listing the sacraments to say: Baptism, Confirmation, First Communion....)

Help your child to realize that he now has a more important place in the worshiping community and that **every** Communion should mean as much to him as his **first** Communion.

With regard to the child's immediate preparation, a few guidelines are listed under "activity" on pp. 198-199. Note the activity book assignment also.

# PREPARATION

## Theme and Aim

We receive Jesus in the spirit of Zacchaeus.
"I will receive Jesus with love and respect."

## Key Words

bow
Amen
Host

## Points for Reflection

— Zacchaeus welcomes Jesus and converts himself (Luke 19:1-10).
— Mary of Bethany joyfully receives Jesus into her house (John 12:1ff.).
— The centurion humbly receives Jesus, declaring his unworthiness (Matthew 8:5ff.).

## Materials

unconsecrated hosts

# PRESENTATION

## Introduction

Spontaneous prayer by teacher or pupil.
After a review of the main points of the last lesson (using the activity book as a guide), you could capitalize on some current event to introduce this new lesson. For example:

Does anybody remember an important person who went to visit our President a few days ago? Was something special done for this important man? *Talk about some of the preparations that are made for important people or even for family guests.*

## Message

Today I will tell you about a visit that **Jesus** paid to someone....

Once there was a man named Zacchaeus, who was not very good. He loved money too much, and he had gotten some of his money unfairly. He had not kept God's rules well.

Zacchaeus had heard about Jesus and he wanted to see Him. One day he heard that Jesus was coming to his city. "Oh, wonderful!" thought Zacchaeus. But when Jesus did arrive in town, there was such a crowd of people around Him that Zacchaeus could not even see Him. Zacchaeus was a short man, you see.

So do you know what he did? He ran on ahead of Jesus and climbed up a big tree by the side of the road. "Now," he said to himself, "I'll be able to see Jesus very well when He comes by."

Jesus came down the road, and Zacchaeus was happy because he could see Him better than almost anyone else could. Suddenly, Jesus lifted His eyes and looked right up at Zacchaeus in the tree!

"Zacchaeus!" He called. "Hurry and come down from the tree, because I am going to stay at your house today!"

How surprised Zacchaeus was! He couldn't believe his ears! **Jesus was coming to his house. Imagine!**

Quick as a flash, Zacchaeus scrambled down the tree and ran home as fast as his short legs would carry him. Everything must be made ready for Jesus' visit. Zacchaeus flew about, ordering his servants to bring out the best food he had and make the house as beautiful as possible.

At last Jesus came, just as He had said He would. Zacchaeus welcomed Him joyfully. He was the happiest man alive that day! Jesus spoke to him kindly, and His eyes looked so loving.

Zacchaeus began to feel very sorry for the way he had offended God. He saw how very good Jesus was, and he wanted to be good, too. So he said to Jesus, "Lord, I will give one half of all my money to the poor people. And if I have cheated someone, I will give him four times what I took from him."

Jesus was very pleased with Zacchaeus! He was very glad that He had gone to Zacchaeus' house. Zacchaeus had given Jesus a wonderful welcome: he had been sorry for offending God and he had promised to become better. This is the best way to welcome Jesus!

Wasn't Zacchaeus lucky to have Jesus come to see him?

But, as far as we know, Zacchaeus saw Jesus only once. Instead, we meet Jesus every time we go to confession. We come close to Him in a special way every time we go into a Catholic church. And in Communion we will welcome Him into our very hearts! We will be able to receive Him every week (and even more often if we are able to go to weekday Masses).

Zacchaeus ran about trying to prepare a very special welcome for Jesus. We can do that, too. For example, we can and should have clean hands and neat clothes. But Jesus was especially pleased when Zacchaeus was sorry for his sins and promised to try to be better. That is what we should especially try to do, just as when we meet Jesus in confession.

Are there times when a person must not go to Communion? Yes, there are. Anyone who has committed a big sin, which we call mortal, must not go to Communion until after telling that sin in confession. *(If he really forgot to tell the sin when going to confession, he could go to Communion, but should tell the sin in his next confession.)*

Also, out of respect for Jesus, we should not eat or drink anything except water or medicine for an hour before Communion. So if a boy or girl ate a candy bar just before Mass, he or she could not go to Communion because Mass usually takes much less than an hour.

*This would be a good time to teach about "spiritual communions," which may be made at any time, in any place.* In a spiritual communion, we can tell Jesus: "Lord Jesus, right now I can't receive You. But please give me Your love and make Your life grow in me. I love You. Please stay with me."

*Discuss making sacrifices in preparation and thanksgiving for Communion, and then speak about prayer:*

There are three important prayers that you can say before Communion, so that you will be more ready to receive Jesus. One is the Our Father. The next is the Lamb of God. We say both of these in the Mass. The third one is a prayer that we **sing** — a song or hymn.

*Show the children the pictures in their textbooks that show how to receive Communion (lesson 19). Read the captions carefully.*

We go up to receive Jesus with our hands folded. Just before our own turn comes, we bow our head out of respect for Jesus. Then we either put out our hands *(demonstrate, showing how to cup the hands slightly)* and say, "Amen," after the priest says, "The body of Christ," or we say "Amen" first and then put out our tongue *(again demonstrate)*. We may receive Communion either way. Whichever way we receive, we should look at the Host while the priest says, "The body of Christ."

*Show the children how to step aside and consume the Host that was received in the hand. Abuses have been noted in this regard, especially among children. It would be well to stress again that the Host is Jesus and that it is to be received as food and at once.*

After we have received the Host, we swallow it as soon as possible. It is all right to chew it if we need to, and if it is stuck in our mouth we can loosen it with our tongue.

*Stress the reverence that should be manifested on the way back to the pew — no unnecessary looking around.*

In the few minutes right after you have received Jesus, you will be very, very close to Him, as close as anyone can be on this earth. You will be richer than a millionnaire, because you will have God Himself right in your heart. Jesus will bring more of His grace, and your soul will shine brightly with it. He will take away some of your faults and give you strength to keep His grace in your soul. He will bless you with His love.

Be sure to thank Him for coming to you! Tell Him, "I love You here in my heart, Jesus. Help me to keep You with me all the time. Bless me, Jesus. Bless my mother and father, bless my brothers and sisters. Bless my teachers, my friends, and everyone I love. Bless everybody in the whole world, dear Jesus! Give us all the grace to be with You one day in heaven."

Ask Jesus to make you good and pleasing to Him always.

Some children say that they have so much to talk about with Jesus that they don't even have enough time. St. Therese used to talk to Him all the way home from church.

## In the Textbook

Read lesson 20.

## REINFORCEMENT

### Summary

We receive Jesus with love and respect. We must have God's grace in us and not have had anything to eat or drink (except water or medicine) for an hour. After Jesus has come to us, we speak with Him heart-to-heart.

### Application

"I will receive Jesus with love and respect."

### Activity

Take the class to church to practice receiving the Eucharist. Explain that the hosts you will use for this practice are only bread. Jesus has not changed them into Himself as He does in the Mass. Explain about the "Amen" that we say in response to the priest's words, "Body of Christ." It is a way of saying, "Yes, I know this is the body of Christ." Show them how to fold their hands, how to bow slightly while the person in front of them is receiving, where to stand when receiving Communion, how to look at the host and receive it properly, how to return to their pews in an orderly fashion without looking around, etc.

Since both options for receiving are in use in your parish, it is well to teach both. However, the children must clearly understand that at any Mass they will receive Jesus in one way or the other; they cannot, for example, receive in the hand and return in a few minutes to receive on the tongue.

A few "don'ts" :

Don't teach the child to close his eyes when receiving, even if he receives on the tongue. He may cause the priest to drop the host.

Don't teach him to bless himself after receiving. He has just received the greatest blessing — God Himself.

Don't forbid him to chew the host. Chewing does not cause pain to the glorified Eucharistic Christ. Also, **do** teach the child how to work the host loose with his tongue if it gets stuck.

Very important — teach him to talk to Jesus in his heart when he has returned to the pew. (This is the point at which he may close his eyes if he wishes.)

## Assignment

Lesson 20 in the activity book.

## ADDITIONAL AIDS AND ACTIVITIES

### In the Classroom

**Banners.** The class could be divided into two groups and make two large banners to be used in the First Communion Mass. Eucharistic symbols — such as chalice and host; wheat and grapes — may be used. Possible quotes: the bread of life (John 6:48). I myself am the living bread (John 6:51).

## At Home

**Learning prayers.** Encourage your child to memorize the brief prayers before and after Communion that he will find in his textbook (after lesson 21). Better still, invite him to make up his own prayers, using those in the text as a guide for content.

## In the Classroom

**Dramatization.** Invite the class to act out the story of Zacchaeus. All those who don't have a main part can belong to the crowd that blocks Zacchaeus' view of Jesus. Each of the children can also accuse Zacchaeus of having cheated him in the past.

# 21

# Holy Communion
# Joins Us Together

## TO PARENTS AND TEACHERS

We should aim at making the Eucharist the center of life for the children, endeavoring to inculcate in them a personal love for Jesus, His Church, and all people. In the *General Catechetical Directory,* we read: "Having been nourished with the Victim of the sacrifice of the Cross, the faithful should by a genuine and active love remove the prejudices because of which they are at times accused of a sterile worship that keeps them from being brotherly and from cooperating with other people. By its nature the Eucharistic banquet is meant to help the faithful to unite their hearts with God more each day in frequent prayer, and thence to acknowledge and love other men as brothers of Christ and sons of God the Father" (n. 58).

## PREPARATION

### Theme and Aim

In Communion Jesus joins us more closely to all the members of His Church and makes us want to love and help everyone.
"I will do a good deed every day."

## Key Words

apostles
Church

## Points for Reflection

— God has willed that all men form one family and deal with each other as brothers (Constitution on the Church in the Modern World, n. 24).

— Christ established charity as the distinctive virtue of His disciples (Decree on the Apostolate of the Laity, n. 8); in fact the first Christians loved each other as brothers (Acts 2:44ff.; 4:32; 11:7ff.).

— In the breaking of the Eucharistic bread, sharing really in the Lord's body, we are raised to communion with Him and among ourselves (Constitution on the Church, n. 7).

— The Eucharistic Celebration must urge us to accomplish works of charity (Decree on the Ministry and Life of Priests, n. 6).

— Spiritual gifts serve nothing without charity (1 Corinthians 13:1-13).

— At the Last Supper, Jesus gave us an example by washing the feet of His disciples. He taught us that the Eucharistic Banquet requires humility and fraternal charity (John 13).

— The Church has us recite the Our Father before Holy Communion to teach us that we cannot approach the Eucharistic meal if we are not sufficiently in peace and charity with our brothers.

## Materials

magazine clippings
scissors
paste
colorful paper
large sheet of paper or cardboard

## PRESENTATION

### *Introduction*

*Our Father.*
*Discuss the opening words of the prayer just said:*
Our **Father.** With God as our Father, we are all — what?
(Brothers and sisters.) We all belong to one big family.
*Ask the children if they have ever gone to a family reunion.*
*Describe what takes place and mention that usually there*
*is at least one meal.*

### *Message*

The Mass is a meal, too. What food do we receive?
*(Wait for response.)* And the Mass is also like a family
reunion. Do you know who the family is?*Explain about the*
*people called the* **Church,** *the family of God's children.*

No matter where we are from or who our parents are,
no matter what the color of our skin, we are all one family
and one people in Jesus Christ.

At the Last Supper, after giving His apostles a new
commandment of love — "Love one another, as I have
loved you" — Jesus said, "If you love me, keep my commandments." You see, children, in order to be saved it
is not enough just to believe what God has taught us
through His Son, Jesus Christ. We must also obey God's
law.

Only when we obey God's commandments do we show
that our love for Him is true.

We find all the commandments of God in the great
commandment of love. Jesus said that the great commandment of love is to love God with our whole heart,
our whole soul, our whole mind and our whole strength —
and to love others as ourselves.

**To love others as ourselves** means: to love everyone
no matter what his race, color or religion; to be polite
and kind on every occasion; to be fair at all times.

To help us understand what He meant by loving our
neighbor, Jesus told stories called parables. This is one
of them:

Once there was a rich man, who wore very nice
clothes and ate very good food every day. And there was

a poor man named Lazarus who didn't own anything at all. He would sit by the gate of the rich man's beautiful home and beg for food. He was sick and covered with sores.

After a while the beggar died. Angels took him to a place of happiness with Abraham, the father of God's people.

Then the rich man died, and he went to hell, a place of fire. From there, he could see Abraham and the beggar Lazarus.

"Father Abraham," called the rich man, "help me. Send Lazarus to bring me even a drop of water. These flames hurt so much."

Do you know what Abraham answered? He said, "My child, remember that during your lifetime you were rich and happy, while Lazarus was poor and sad. Now he has found happiness, but you are in pain."

Then the rich man asked Abraham to send Lazarus to warn the rich man's brothers about hell. But Abraham answered that the rich man's brothers should already know how to avoid hell because they knew God's law — the ten commandments.

From this story we see that the rich man was punished because he had not kept God's commandments about loving others. He had been very selfish, enjoying himself without ever helping Lazarus and other poor people who needed help. Let us remember that God expects us to be good to everyone.

*Talk about how the children can help others.*

## In the Textbook

*Read lesson 21.*

## REINFORCEMENT

### Summary

We belong to Jesus' great family, the Church. In Communion, He joins us more closely to everyone in the Church and makes us want to love and help everybody.

## Application

"I will do a good deed every day."

## Activity

*Invite the children to make a large collage showing our oneness in Christ. A chalice and host (see chalice patterns in this manual) may be surrounded by magazine clippings of all sorts of people mounted on colorful paper.*

## Assignment

*Lesson 21 in the activity book. The children may need help.*

## ADDITIONAL AIDS AND ACTIVITIES

### At Home

**Mass check.** Note what your child understands about the Mass. Help him to deepen his understanding by reviewing the preceding lessons with him.

### At Home

**Communion breakfast.** If possible, receive Holy Communion as a family and hold a "family Communion breakfast" afterwards to emphasize the unity brought about by the Sacrament of Love. (Before eating you might read portions of John 6.)

# 22
# With Jesus We Walk
# Toward Heaven

## TO PARENTS AND TEACHERS

In their simple, pure faith the children *can become* profoundly aware of the real presence of Jesus among us, and of how to live a truly Eucharistic life. Stress Christ's immense love, reminding them that children are His favorites. It will not be difficult, then, to stir up feelings of gratitude and love.

## PREPARATION

### Theme and Aim

Jesus is with us to give us strength on our journey towards heaven. He remains in our churches in the Holy Eucharist, also called the Blessed Sacrament.

"I will visit Jesus often."

### Key Words

tabernacle
Blessed Sacrament
adore
offend
Pope

## Points for Reflection

—*The miraculous bread given by the angel to Elijah is a figure of the Eucharist (1 Kings 19:1-8).*

—*In the earthly liturgy we have a foretaste of that heavenly liturgy which is celebrated in the holy city of Jerusalem, toward which we journey as pilgrims, where Christ is sitting at the right hand of God, a minister of the holies and the true tabernacle (Constitution on the Sacred Liturgy, n. 8; Constitution on the Church, n. 50).*

—*With the visit to the Blessed Sacrament the faithful respond with gratitude to the gift of Him who continually remains in our midst in our churches (Decree on the Ministry and Life of Priests, n. 5).*

—*The Eucharistic Visit is a proof of our thankfulness, a sign of love and debt of gratitude to Christ the Lord, present in the tabernacle (Paul VI, Mystery of Faith).*

## Materials

*optional* —
filmstrip-cassette "St. Tarcisius"

# PRESENTATION

## Introduction

*Glory to the Father....*

*Drawing on some well-known event, such as a march to benefit the poor, a footrace, a mountain climbing expedition...ask the children what these people do soon afterwards.* (They drink and eat.) Why do they do that? (They need to get their strength back.)

## Message

*Make the comparison with Communion—we nourish ourselves with the Eucharist because our journey through life wears us out spiritually. We need to get back our spiritual strength in order to stay good and become better.*

We receive strength from Jesus through Communion and confession. But suppose there was a day that you hadn't been able to receive Communion or go to confession. Is there something you could do to receive strength from Jesus? *Lead the class to the thought of praying, and in particular of praying in church, before the Blessed Sacrament. Also review how to make spiritual communions.*

*Turn in the textbook to the pages about prayer before the Blessed Sacrament. (These follow lesson 22.) Read them over together and discuss their meaning.*

*You might then show or tell the story of St. Tarcisius, to bring home the reality of the Eucharistic presence. Tarcisius gave up his life because he did not want the Eucharist to be profaned:*

In the early years of the Church, some people who didn't believe in Jesus used to put Jesus' followers in prison and even kill them.

Because of this, Jesus' followers in the city of Rome used to go down into underground tunnels called catacombs and have Mass in secret. The catacomb tunnels stretched for miles in all directions, so the Christians felt safer having Mass down there than in their homes. (There were no church buildings yet, because the rulers of Rome did not believe in Jesus and did not want other people to follow Him.)

*At this point, if you have the sound filmstrip St. Tarcisius, show it to the children. If you do not have the filmstrip, you might continue with the following narration:*

The Pope, leader of the whole Church, used to celebrate Mass in the catacombs, too. One day, Tarcisius, a boy only a few years older than you are, was there at the Pope's Mass. After Mass the Pope asked, "Would anyone here be willing to bring the Holy Eucharist to our friends in prison?"

This was a very dangerous errand, because the person bringing the Eucharist might be put into prison, too. Yet it was important for the Holy Eucharist to be brought to the prisoners. Do you know why? *Wait for response.* The prisoners were going to be killed for following Jesus, and they needed the strength Jesus gives in Communion in order to die for Him.

"I will carry the Holy Eucharist," said Tarcisius.

The Pope was surprised, because Tarcisius was only a boy. But then he agreed. After all, a boy might not be suspected. He might have a better chance of bringing the Holy Eucharist into the prison.

So the Pope hung the little case that contained the Hosts on a chain around the boy's neck. And Tarcisius started out for the prison.

He walked quickly, without looking around.

"Tarcisius, come play with us," shouted a boy he knew.

"I can't—sorry!" Tarcisius called back. He kept on walking. A group of boys came running after him and surrounded him.

"What have you got there?" they asked. Tarcisius pressed both hands tightly around the case containing the consecrated Hosts. He didn't answer, because none of these boys was a follower of Jesus. They would not understand that the Eucharist is Jesus Himself and that It must be treated with great respect.

"He's carrying the mysteries!" someone shouted. "Mysteries" was the word everyone used for the Eucharist.

The boys closed in on Tarcisius and tried to pull the case out of his hands. But he wouldn't let go, because he knew that if he **did** they would tear open the case and do to the Holy Eucharist the worst things they could think of.

"Jesus," he prayed, "make me strong enough to hold on."

And Jesus gave him the strength. The boys couldn't force his hands open. Finally someone picked up a stone and hit Tarcisius. Another boy did the same. Suddenly all of them backed off and formed a ring, pelting him with stones from all sides. Tarcisius fell to the ground, bleeding badly.

"Out of the way! What's all this?" A big soldier pushed his way through the group of boys. "Get out of here!" he ordered. The boys looked at him and then at Tarcisius.

They could see that they had hurt Tarcisius very badly, and suddenly they were afraid. The soldier could punish them for what they had done! Suddenly they all ran away, leaving the soldier there with Tarcisius.

The soldier, whose name was Quadratus, knew Tarcisius. Quadratus, too, was a follower of Jesus. He knelt down beside the bleeding boy. Tarcisius was unconscious. But his hands still held the little case tightly.

Quadratus picked up Tarcisius and carried him to the home of a good Christian woman he knew.

In the woman's house, Tarcisius regained consciousness for a few moments. "I have the Eucharist here," he said. "Tell the Pope that I kept it safe and didn't let them take it."

Then Tarcisius died, knowing that the Holy Eucharist was safe with his friends.

Ever since that time the Church has honored Tarcisius as a **saint** — a special friend of God in heaven.

## In the Textbook

*Read lesson 22.*

## REINFORCEMENT

### Summary

Jesus in the Eucharist gives us strength to reach heaven. Jesus is always with us, especially in the Holy Eucharist, which we also call the Blessed Sacrament.

### Application

"I will visit Jesus often."

### Activity

*Take the class to pay a brief visit to the Blessed Sacrament, in which the children sing a Eucharistic hymn, such as "I Am the Bread of Life," and pray silently, thank-*

*ing Jesus for the great gift of Himself that He has left us in the Eucharist. This brief silent prayer (2 or 3 minutes) could be followed by recitation of the prayers for a visit to the Blessed Sacrament that they will find in their textbooks (after chapter 22).*

## Assignment

*Lesson 22 in the activity book.*

## ADDITIONAL AIDS AND ACTIVITIES

### In the Classroom

**Mural or series of posters.** The story of St. Tarcisius. Backgrounds for the various scenes could be made by dabbing with a paper towel that has been dipped in paint. The figures could be silhouettes cut or torn from construction paper.

### At Home or in the Classroom

**"Creed."** Help the children compile a list of truths they already know. For example: "I know that God loves me. I know that God is my Father. I know that I became God's child in Baptism...."

# 23
# Mary, Model of Every Friend of Jesus

## TO PARENTS AND TEACHERS

This Penance-Eucharist program concludes with a lesson on devotion to the Blessed Virgin, for Mary is "the path that leads to Christ." Love for Mary assures fervent and frequent reception of Penance and Eucharist. It is a mark of an authentic Catholic Christian.

## PREPARATION

### Theme and Aim

Mary, the Mother of Jesus, is our example in following Him.

"I will pray to Mary every day."

### Key Words

hail
blessed

### Points for Reflection

— Mary listened to the words of the angel Gabriel and responded that she was ready to do the will of God (Luke 1:26-38).

*—Mary loved her neighbors, and for this reason she hastened to her cousin Elizabeth to help her (Luke 1:39-45).*

*—Mary listened to the words of God, meditated on them in her heart and put them into practice (Luke 2:21-40, 2:41-52, 11:27-28).*

*—Mary remained faithful to God in spite of sufferings (Luke 2:21-40, 2:13-15; John 19:17-34).*

*—Mary is the perfect model of faith, of hope, of charity and of every other virtue. She is the faithful instrument in the hands of God to cooperate in the work of redemption. She is the Mother of God and our mother, helping us on our journey toward heaven (Constitution on the Church, nn. 52-69).*

## Materials

picture or statue of Mary

# PRESENTATION

## Introduction

*Spontaneous prayer, followed by a silent spiritual communion.*

*Ask questions based on the activity book homework.*

## Message

*Display a picture or statue of the Blessed Virgin. Ask who she is and what prayer to her we know.*

Mary is the Mother of Jesus. And Jesus is God. So Mary is God's own Mother! And Jesus, our Brother, wants Mary to be our Mother, too.

Do you know that God did something wonderful for Mary? Yes, He did! Because she was to be the Mother of His Son, He made her free from original sin right from the first moment of her life. She always had God's grace in her. This is a very special privilege that God gave to the Blessed Virgin Mary. We call this very special privilege Mary's Immaculate Conception.

Would you like to hear about a fourteen-year-old girl who had the wonderful privilege of seeing the Blessed Mother?

St. Bernadette was born into a very poor family. Very often they did not have enough bread to eat or even wood to light the fire. Bernadette went many times to hunt for wood with her sisters and friends.

One day, while they were looking for wood, a beautiful Lady suddenly appeared to Bernadette. The Lady was dressed in white. She had a blue ribbon about her waist and a rose on her feet. She was a very, very beautiful Lady!

Bernadette was surprised and just a bit afraid. Who was it? From where had she come?

After a minute of silence, Bernadette asked the lovely Lady, "Who are you?"

The Lady did not answer, but she had such a beautiful smile on her lips that Bernadette could not take her eyes from her.

The Lady invited Bernadette to go to that place again on other days. She told her the exact hour to go, and she promised that she would be there every time.

Bernadette went. She saw the beautiful Lady eighteen times.

The last time, she begged, "Please, beautiful Lady, tell me who you are!"

The Lady answered, "I am the Immaculate Conception."

It was the Blessed Mother! The Immaculate Conception!

In the place where the Immaculate Conception had appeared many times, a place called Lourdes, France, a great church was built. Many people go there to pray to the Blessed Mother. Many sick people are cured when they go to Lourdes.

Why does Jesus do these wonderful things when people pray to His Mother? Because He loves her so. She is the most wonderful mother there ever was. What good care she took of Him when He was born! How she adored

Him and loved Him! No other person was ever as faithful to God as Mary was. No one, except Jesus, ever obeyed the Father as well as Mary did. No wonder Jesus loves her with all His heart! No wonder He likes us to pray to Mary.

Mary teaches us all the things we need to know to be true children of God. If we pray to her and imitate her, she will show us how to be good members of the Church and faithful children of God so that we can reach our home in heaven.

The Blessed Mother is **our** Mother. She loves us very much. She asks God to give us many graces and blessings. She always hears our prayers.

There was a little Japanese boy named Kazno who was going to religion class.

*If there is a map available or a globe, point Japan out. Show how far it is from our country. Point out that the Church of Jesus is all over the world. You do the mission cause a great service if you interest your young pupils in the spreading of the Faith.*

Kazno was not a Catholic, but the missionary Sister who taught the class was happy to prepare Kazno for his baptism. One day the little boy came late to class. "Mama is sick!" he said. "They took her away to the hospital!" The Sister tried to calm Kazno down and comfort him. As the days passed, his mother grew worse and worse. Poor Kazno! He was so sad! His house seemed so empty without his mother.

One morning, right in the middle of class, Kazno stood up and pointed to a picture of the Blessed Mother hanging above the teacher's desk. "If my mother had a picture of Maria-Sama, she would certainly get better!" he cried. "Maria-Sama" means the Blessed Mother for the Japanese.

When Kazno left school that very day, he had a beautiful picture of Mary under his arm. It was a picture of Mary Immaculate, as she appeared to St. Bernadette. Kazno looked happy for the first time in a long time. Sister had said that Mary is our heavenly Mother, who always helps us. He felt sure that Mary would help his mother get well again.

Do you think Kazno was .right?... Yes, indeed! Soon enough, his mother was well and strong again! And do you know what else happened? Kazno's mother went to see the Sister who gave Kazno the picture of Mary. "Thank you so much!" she said. "Maria-Sama's smile seemed to help me get well. And now I want to learn more about her. Please tell me about her and her Son Jesus!"

Listen, children, to the wonderful way things turned out: Kazno's mother and his father and his sister all took instructions about our Catholic Faith, and they all were baptized! See what the Blessed Mother did,. all because a little boy trusted in her!

*Encourage the children to develop the habit of praying often to Jesus and Mary.*

When we pray, God's life in us grows. We find it easier to be good, and to keep close to Jesus. We find it easier to be a loving child of God, a kind, helpful "neighbor" like the good Samaritan Jesus told us about. It is not at all hard to pray.

There are some nice short prayers which you might like to say often. They take just a minute. One of them is, "My Jesus, mercy." Another is, "Most Sacred Heart of Jesus, have mercy on us." In these prayers we ask Jesus to forgive us and help us. You may even make up your own little prayers, like this: "Jesus, I love You! Make me good!"

Jesus and His Blessed Mother are very pleased with these little prayers. You don't have to kneel down to say them. You can say them anywhere, not only in church, even though church is the best place. You can pray anywhere, at any time. As you walk along the street, as you dry dishes for mother, or even when you are outdoors playing with your friends, you can always think of Jesus a minute and say, "Most Sacred Heart of Jesus, have mercy on us," or any other little prayer.

This is the way to keep close to Jesus and to keep out of sin. I know of big workingmen who say many little prayers during the day. I know a policeman who carries a rosary in his glove. He prays while he directs traffic on a busy street. Mothers at home pray while they do their housework. We pray when we are happy, to thank our good God. We pray when we are sad, to ask His help. We pray when we feel tempted to sin, when we don't know what to do, when we need something. Those who pray much are the happiest people, because they are never lonely. They keep close to God.

## In the Textbook

*Read lesson 23.*

## REINFORCEMENT

### Summary

Mary is Jesus' Mother and His most faithful follower. She is our model in following Jesus. We pray to Mary especially with the Hail Mary.

### Application

"I will pray to Mary every day."

### Assignment

*Lesson 23 in the activity book.*

## ADDITIONAL AIDS AND ACTIVITIES

### At Home or in the Classroom

**Marian Shrine.** A simple, effective background for a statue of the Blessed Virgin can be made from stiff, colored paper.

First, take a large rectangle of scrap paper, which will become your pattern. Fold it like this and cut a slit in the middle of the short, folded part:

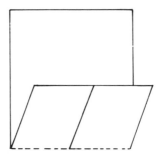

Next, fold the pattern again—this time, lengthwise—and cut as shown:

Open the pattern and stand it up like this:

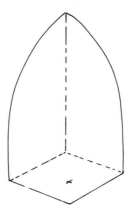

Check its height and general shape against your statue and make the necessary corrections.

Trace the opened pattern onto your good paper. (The shrine will look nicer if you do not fold the good paper lengthwise as was done with the pattern. But cut the slit for folding the base.)

A staple joining the two halves of the base together at the spot marked "X" in the sketch will hold the shrine in the desired position.

## In the Classroom

**Marian Celebration.** At the beginning of this celebration, the children (walking around the classroom in procession as they sing a Marian song or hymn) could place the statue of our Lady in the shrine, with flowers on either side.

*Teacher:* Because Jesus loves us so much, He gave us His own holy Mother to be our own Mother. Mary loves us very much. She always hears our prayers. When we pray to her, she brings us closer to Jesus. Please stand to listen to a reading from the holy Gospel according to Luke.

*Reading:* (Luke 2:42-52)
This is the Gospel of the Lord.

*Class:* Praise to You, Lord Jesus Christ.

*Teacher:* From this reading we can see how much Mary loved Jesus. Mary loves us, too. We should pray to her often. Let us stand now and respond: My soul praises the Lord.

*Class:* My soul praises the Lord.

*Teacher:* Praise the Lord for He is good.

*Class:* My soul praises the Lord.

*Teacher:* Sing praise to our God for He is loving.

*Class:* My soul praises the Lord.

*Teacher:* It is right for us to praise Him.

*Class:* My soul praises the Lord.

*Teacher:* The Lord be with you.

*Class:* And also with you.

*Teacher:* A reading from the holy Gospel according to John.

*Class:*     Glory to You, Lord.
*Teacher:*  (John 2:1-11)
            This is the Gospel of the Lord.
*Class:*     Praise to You, Lord Jesus Christ.
*Homily:*   *You may wish to give a brief homily pointing out that Jesus, who is God, helped the people His Mother wanted Him to help. When we pray to Mary, she asks Jesus to help us.*

   *Hymn to Mary*
*Teacher:* Let us pray to the Lord our God, responding:
            Lord, hear our prayer.
*Class:*     Lord, hear our prayer.
*Teacher:* That Mary will teach us how to love Jesus, we
            pray to the Lord.
*Class:*     Lord, hear our prayer.
*Teacher:* That Mary will ask Jesus to help us, we pray to
            the Lord.
*Class:*     Lord, hear our prayer.
*Teacher:* Now let us pray all together to Mary our Mother:
*Class:*     Hail Mary . . . .

**BOOKS & MEDIA**

*The Daughters of St. Paul operate book and media centers at the following addresses. Visit, call or write the one nearest you today, or find us on the World Wide Web, www.pauline.org*

**CALIFORNIA**
3908 Sepulveda Blvd., Culver City, CA 90230; 310-397-8676
5945 Balboa Ave., San Diego, CA 92111; 858-565-9181
46 Geary Street, San Francisco, CA 94108; 415-781-5180

**FLORIDA**
145 S.W. 107th Ave., Miami, FL 33174; 305-559-6715

**HAWAII**
1143 Bishop Street, Honolulu, HI 96813; 808-521-2731
Neighbor Islands call: 800-259-8463

**ILLINOIS**
172 North Michigan Ave., Chicago, IL 60601; 312-346-4228

**LOUISIANA**
4403 Veterans Memorial Blvd., Metairie, LA 70006; 504-887-7631

**MASSACHUSETTS**
Rte. 1, 885 Providence Hwy., Dedham, MA 02026; 781-326-5385

**MISSOURI**
9804 Watson Rd., St. Louis, MO 63126; 314-965-3512

**NEW JERSEY**
561 U.S. Route 1, Wick Plaza, Edison, NJ 08817; 732-572-1200

**NEW YORK**
150 East 52nd Street, New York, NY 10022; 212-754-1110
78 Fort Place, Staten Island, NY 10301; 718-447-5071

**OHIO**
2105 Ontario Street, Cleveland, OH 44115; 216-621-9427

**PENNSYLVANIA**
9171-A Roosevelt Blvd., Philadelphia, PA 19114; 215-676-9494

**SOUTH CAROLINA**
243 King Street, Charleston, SC 29401; 843-577-0175

**TENNESSEE**
4811 Poplar Ave., Memphis, TN 38117; 901-761-2987

**TEXAS**
114 Main Plaza, San Antonio, TX 78205; 210-224-8101

**VIRGINIA**
1025 King Street, Alexandria, VA 22314; 703-549-3806

**CANADA**
3022 Dufferin Street, Toronto, Ontario, Canada M6B 3T5; 416-781-9131
1155 Yonge Street, Toronto, Ontario, Canada M4T 1W2; 416-934-3440

¡También somos su fuente para libros, videos y música en español!